O9-ABI-186

HEGEMONY AND SPORT

POWER THROUGH CULTURE IN THEORY AND PRACTICE

HEGEMONY AND SPORT

POWER THROUGH CULTURE IN THEORY AND PRACTICE

APRIL HENNING AND JESPER ANDREASSON

First published in 2022
as part of the *Sport and Society* Book Imprint
doi: 10.18848/978-1-957792-14-9/CGP (Full Book)

Common Ground Research Networks
University of Illinois Research Park
2001 South First St, Suite 201 L
Champaign, IL 61820 USA

Copyright © [April Henning, Jesper Andreasson] 2022
All rights reserved. Apart from fair dealing for the purposes of study, research, criticism or review as
permitted under the applicable copyright legislation, no part of this book may be reproduced by any process
without written permission from the publisher.

Library of Congress Cataloging-in-Publication Data

Names: Henning, April, author. | Andreasson, Jesper, author.
Title: Hegemony and Sport : Power Through Culture in Theory and Practice /
  April Henning, Jesper Andreasson.
Description: Champaign, IL : Common Ground Research Networks, 2022. |
  Series: Sport & Society Teaching Pocketbook Series; vol. 1 | Includes
  bibliographical references. | Summary: "How does power work in sport,
  especially when there seems to be no one enforcing unspoken rules? One
  way of analyzing power is through the concept of hegemony - a soft form
  of power exercised through consent rather than force, through ongoing
  interaction between the powerful and powerless to produce common sense
  understandings of society and culture. This book focuses on how hegemony
  works, particularly in sport, to understand how power, dominance, and
  resistance may manifest in different ways within a variety of sport
  contexts, in theory and practice. It also discusses how hegemony can
  work within sport and how dominance and power are maintained - as well
  as sometimes being challenged or resisted. Through discussions to help
  students develop tools for analyzing issues of power and empirical
  examples that show how various concepts can bring a deepened
  understanding of sport and society, this book gives insight into
  hegemony in sport"-- Provided by publisher.
Identifiers: LCCN 2022038661 (print) | LCCN 2022038662 (ebook) | ISBN
  9781957792200 (paperback) | ISBN 9781957792217 (pdf)
Subjects: LCSH: Sports--Social aspects. | Sports administration--Social
  aspects. | Hegemony. | Masculinity in sports. | Team sports. | World
  Anti-Doping Agency.
Classification: LCC GV706.5 .H457 2022 (print) | LCC GV706.5 (ebook) |
  DDC 306.4/83--dc23/eng/20220923
LC record available at https://lccn.loc.gov/2022038661
LC ebook record available at https://lccn.loc.gov/2022038662

Editorial Assitant: Patricia Alonso Membrilla

SPORT & SOCIETY POCKETBOOK TEACHING SERIES

The **Sport and Society Pocketbook Teaching Series** aims to introduce students and a general readership to relevant topics, theories, and concepts within sport history and sport sociology. The topics will vary but are united in their purpose to serve as an accessible alternative to generic textbook offerings or academic research monographs. We hope that the shorter and more accessible pocketbook format of the series will mean that each book can be read in an hour or two on a quiet evening or while commuting on a bus or train. This aligns with our ethos of accessibility in scholarly communication.

Books in the series can be accessed in print and electronic formats. In addition, and in parallel to both editions, each title will be accompanied by an online repository where additional learning and teaching resources are provided. The electronic platform for the series will include links to recent and significant research articles, visual materials, podcasts, lectures, and more, thus securing ongoing relevance by providing new and engaging resources and perspectives aligned with the topic of each book.

This series is for teachers, learners, and individuals with an interest in sports alike.

Dr. Jörg Krieger (Aarhus University, Denmark)
Dr. April Henning (University of Stirling, United Kingdom)
Dr. Lindsay Parks Pieper (University of Lynchburg, United States)
Dr. Jesper Andreasson (Linnaeus University, Sweden)

A link to access additional online resources is provided at:
https://doi.org/10.18848/978-1-957792-21-7/CGP

TABLE OF CONTENTS

INTRODUCTION

What do you think of when you hear the word **power**? Maybe you think of the power of your government to determine the amount of tax you pay or the amounts of funding schools and parks receive. Possibly you think of military power or the power of the police to stop you if you drive too fast. You could think of the power of protestors to convince policymakers to change things, such as how women (and men) have fought for various rights throughout history. On a more personal level, you might think of the power your lecturer has over your course grade, the power your parents had over your bedtime when you were young, or bullies who made life difficult in adolescence. Each of these examples represents a type of power and a relationship based on a particular dynamic. Such dynamics occur between countries and institutions, and across levels, such as structural, cultural, and individual.

There are many different definitions of and approaches to power. One basic and common approach is that power includes the idea of an individual, institution, or even a country with the ability to get others to do what they want (Dahl 1957). Power is about influence, and the ability to discipline, control, and steer the actions, and even the thoughts, of others. This can be done in many different ways. Sometimes the way power operates is very clear and easily understood from the time we are children. For example, when someone breaks the law, power may manifest in the punishment that follows. Through the work of the police, lawyers, judges, and others, the justice system upholds the social order, as well as controls and exercises direct or hard power over citizens (Barnett and Duvall 2005).

But what about power that we cannot really see or might not even be fully aware of? In that case it is a different type of power operating. This is what has been referred to as *productive power* (Foucault 1980). This type of power can still direct our behaviors, views, and beliefs, but it operates on a cultural level and often does not require laws or formal enforcement. It is productive in the sense that it produces people who behave in specified ways, making it seem as if these behaviors and beliefs come from within. Through socialization we have gained an understanding of culture in which we live. As a result, we have learned on a grand scale to accept and expect that everyone will share some views and ways of doing things. These norms and values often tend to privilege a certain group in society. It can be the rich and wealthy over the poor, men over women, etc.

Power can also be a question of culture and ideals. This kind of power does not concern things we are punished for directly if we do not comply, but it does concern many things that we might expect to see around us or things that are expected of us. For example, why are we not surprised to see American fast food chains almost everywhere we travel around the world? Or why do we assume that the nuclear family of a mother, father, and children is the default family unit? Further, why do many think some sports are more suited to boys than girls? These ideas and experiences are dominant in society, and they influence our ideas and assumptions when we think about how things should be or how we expect them to be. We might even think that some things really should be different, yet still take the status quo for granted.

When the norms and values of one group dominate in a given society we have what we call **hegemonic power** or **hegemony** — a collective and softer power exercised more through consent than force and that operates through ongoing interaction between the powerful and powerless to produce common sense understandings of society and culture (Haugaard and Lentner 2006; Gallarotti 2011). Sport is one social arena where this type of power functions and produces particular dynamics and beliefs. This happens through practices on fields and pitches, in locker room talk, and when youngsters (or their parents) choose to engage in one sport and not the other due to gender, ethnicity, or even social class (Rowe 2004).

This book looks at how hegemony works, particularly in sport. Our main focus is on how power, dominance, and resistance may manifest in different ways and on different levels within a variety of sport contexts. More precisely, we will discuss and show how hegemony can work within sport and how dominance and power are maintained, as well as sometimes challenged or resisted. We will do this through discussions that will help you develop tools for analyzing issues of power, and through empirical examples that show how various concepts can bring a deepened understanding of sport and society. First, though, we will consider two of the key concepts associated with hegemony: power and culture. In order to understand the concept of hegemony as both a lens and a theoretical tool, we must first consider how it relates to other forms of power and its potential applications.

Early Sociological Approaches To Power

As noted above, there are different types of power and these have led to different definitions and understandings of the concept. Indeed, questions of power have been central in sociological thinking for a long time and have influenced scholars in their ambitions to understand culture and the relationship between the individual and society; the free will of the individual versus institutional control. The German sociologist **Max Weber**, for example, wrote extensively about the related ideas of power and authority (see: Weber 1962; 2009). He defined power simply as the ability of an actor (person or institution) to achieve what it wants even when there are others trying to prevent it. Within this direct and hard form of power, he then identified two distinct types of power: *coercive* and *authoritative*. Coercive power means using force to get someone to do something. The use of — or threat of — violence or other physical duress is a very clear and basic form of direct power that has been leveraged by countries, criminals, even school bullies. This form of power can be either legitimate or illegitimate — that is, it can be viewed as proper and allowable or as unacceptable.

Authoritative power is that which is legitimate on its face because those who are subject to that power have consented to it in some way. Weber identified three forms of authoritative power: *traditional*, *charismatic*, and *rational-legal*. Traditional authority is power that is customarily held and passed on through inheritance. Family-based monarchies where power and position are handed down from parents to children are based on traditional authority. By contrast, charismatic authority is based on the personality or qualities of a specific leader who uses those to influence others. Some examples might be a particularly likable politician who uses their charm to get votes, or a charming and well-spoken religious leader who is able to communicate their views to their followers and guide their behaviors. Rational-legal authority is based on the position held by the person or institution to tell others what to do. Judges who gain the right to make legal judgment in courts have that power based on their position within the judicial system.

Weber was mostly talking about the power of states, governments, or leaders over society and other groups. These types of power and relationships are important to understand and analyze, but they are a bit limited as they tend to focus on power that operates in only one top-down direction. There are also those who have looked at other power relationships and directions through which it works, such as that between different economic groups or cultures.

Karl Marx was a critical theorist who focused on the conditions of laborers as a result of their position relative to the upper classes. Marx was politically engaged but here we will focus on his scientific contributions and how he analyzed society (see: Marx 2013 [1848]; Marx and Engels 2009). According to Marx, the ruling class (bourgeoisie) stood in opposition to the laboring class (proletariat). The bourgeoisie's power lay in its control of the means of production — meaning they controlled the how, when, and what of industry — while the proletariat simply sold their manual labor. Power, then, is located in economics and rooted in materialism — the view that material things or money are valued above all else. This economic power is held and used by the upper class to determine and reinforce the values and lifestyles of the upper class and to control the proletariat. This top-down form of power then determined culture, as the upper ruling class propagated its ideas and ideals to the lower classes. Power in Marx's view was limited in supply and a negative force, used as a tool of one group to oppress and control another. This is done not only through economic power but also as a consequence of spreading cultural ideals influencing how people think about the world. This might include the structure of family life, education, or what to strive for in life. The result is that we can see how an economic system — a capitalist system — tends to influence culture and society and allows those at the top of the system to hold power over increasingly alienated citizens at the bottom.

Others have taken analyses of power in still different directions. The French philosopher **Michel Foucault**, was mainly interested in how power operates in various directions in society (see: Foucault 1979; 1980), such as through peer groups such as between athletes on a team, members of a church, or coworkers. In this view, these relationships are what ultimately allow societies to be controlled. Power is not something oppressive reserved for governments or policymakers. Rather, it is based in relationships at multiple levels, including the individual level, and is wielded by everyone. This kind of power is positive, in that it aims to produce subjects or citizens who conform with and police themselves according to social norms through disciplining processes. Foucault used the philosopher Jeremy Bentham's model of the Panopticon. The Panopticon was conceived as a model of prison surveillance, with an all-seeing guard tower in the center. Because the prisoners could not know when or if they were being monitored, they would need to behave in accordance with the rules of the prison at all times. Eventually, the prisoners internalized this gaze, meaning they began to guard and supervise their own behavior. Foucault translated this into broader society, exploring how social institutions (e.g., churches, schools, sports) disciplined both minds and bodies to conform to social and cultural expectations. Control became self-control and individuals became responsible for ensuring conformity with social and cultural norms. One function of this kind of power comes from redefining social issues (i.e., drug addiction) as individual responsibilities (i.e., "Just say no" campaigns). By transforming these issues into questions of personal choice and responsibility, failures to conform become the fault of individual rather than of the state or society to provide adequate support and resources to address the broader, underlying causes.

Weber, Marx, and Foucault are only a few important examples of how issues of power and dominance have been addressed through classic sociological theory. Though they have somewhat different perspectives and use different approaches to understand power, there are still some similarities in their aims. Each had something to say about society and culture, and about the role of the individual in a system that serves to control or steer minds and bodies in certain directions.

Culture: Symbols, Language And The Ordering Of Life

Just as power is a complicated and somewhat multilayered concept, there is no universal definition of what culture is and how it should be understood. In their analyses, various scholars have tended to focus on different and somewhat limited aspects of culture (Billington et al. 1991). For example, much interest has been shown in topics such as how lifestyles and ideals are formed by culture, struggles over cultural ideals, and the relationship between common culture and various subcultures (Williams 2011). Approaching the concept of culture broadly there are also some commonalities between explanations by various scholars. Roughly, culture can be understood as an umbrella term for the norms, ideals, and values that underpin a group or society. These then guide individuals' actions or practices, through which culture is often expressed. Cultural ideas are often taken for granted by members of a group, as they become internalized and routine. Then in turn, practices become reminders of culture, reinforcing those norms and values. For example, aggressive play is part of ice hockey culture and expected by players and spectators; each aggressive game then reinforces this aspect of ice hockey culture — and potentially normative understandings of masculinity as well. Culture, then, can be understood as relating to the expectations, customs, and social behaviors within a particular group of people.

Cultures also include material things. The value placed on material things can vary greatly by culture, which may itself vary greatly based on the environment in which it exists. In coastal areas, culture may be expressed through owning specific kinds of boats and consumption of fresh seafood, whereas in urban areas material culture might entail cars or designer office clothes. Further, culture is largely a question of symbols, of which our most important system of symbols is language. A culture is formed and partially transmitted through language. The way we talk, what we joke about, and even what we avoid discussing with others is part of culture. Thus, when we learn language we also learn culture. To this end, culture can be understood as sort of a scheme or a map through which we decipher and interpret our world and society. That is, through culture we learn to interpret the world in a particular way. We learn to distinguish good from bad, masculinity from femininity, civilized from uncivilized, clean from dirty, and more.

Through language we learn culture, which helps us to categorize experiences. To some extent, culture allows daily life to become predictable and safe. Culture creates order, which can be understood as sort of a social rhythm in a group. For example, cultures help individuals know what is expected of them and what the social dynamic in a particular culture setting looks like. Culture serves to counter a sense of chaos and disorder, as well as creates a sense of stability in society. It works as an anchor to places, communities, and groups, providing the foundation for interactions and behaviors that become part of everyday life.

But culture is also demanding. We interpret not only the actions of others through culture, we also employ cultural understandings to determine our own actions. Culture provides a lens through which we learn to interpret our surroundings. In this way, culture can hardly be distinguished from the exercise of power. In cultures where money and wealth are highly valued, those without these resources may be looked down upon by others or view themselves as lacking compared to their wealthy counterparts. This also applies to sport. If we, for example, operate in a culture in which it is considered central to take care of one's body and health, or to have a body that looks a certain way, people who fail to live up to such ideals may be questioned and even ridiculed. Some may even themselves feel as failures for not being able to live up to dominant cultural ideals. To this end, culture is very much a tool for influencing people in certain directions. Culture is power and power is exercised through culture.

The Dynamic Relationship Between Culture And Power: The "Birth" Of Hegemony

Sociologist, historians, sport scientists, and, of course, a wide variety of scholars from other fields and disciplines, have long paid attention to how power and dominance operate in and through culture and society. Within the social sciences, questions of power, as well as resistance to it, have long been a central feature in analyses of not only social structures, but also in people's daily lives. The concepts to understand such systems and expressions of power have varied. For example, one term often used to describe men´s general power over women, which manifests in and through culture, is *patriarchy*. This term has served to describe structural conditions through which men/fathers can dominate family life in different ways and hold privileged positions in society, thereby also oppressing women as a collective.

But certainly, power and dominance are not always this clear cut. Rather, social life is often more dynamic and complex, as is culture. As explained above, power can be expressed and exercised in practices, as well as through cultural ideals that serve to benefit one group and disadvantage others. People — no matter their sex, age, ethnicity, sexuality, etc. — cannot be understood as ruled by force alone; they are also directed through ideas and the pervasive power of ideology, beliefs, and values that serve to form minds and shape practices through culture. There is also a constant battle over culture and cultural values. This battle may take many forms and cuts across different categories. In pre-industrial society for example, culture largely focused on things like natural resources, seasons of the year, and livestock farming. This culture was dominant as many societies revolved around agriculture and agrarian life. But following industrialization, people gradually started to move into the cities and engaging in wage labor. A new urban culture was on the rise, providing alternative values, dynamics, and lifestyles. Urbanites were making claims of cultural power and dominance. Following this, new ideals were formed and much pre-industrial culture was successively replaced, which meant that new understandings of labor, time, leisure, and more were implemented. As a result, a more dynamic approach to understanding and analyzing the relationship between power and culture is found in the concept of *hegemony* (Howson and Smith 2012).

Hegemony As Concept And Theory: What To Expect

The title of this book is *Hegemony and Sport*. These two concepts will be at the center of attention throughout, but in slightly different ways. Hegemony is a theoretical or analytical concept, a tool for understanding something. Sport is a context for application, or the place where what we want to understand exists or is happening. We will use the concept of hegemony as a way of looking at and analyzing sport as: 1) a phenomenon, 2) a lived practice or set of experiences, and 3) as a producer of culture and cultural beliefs. We will discuss and illustrate how hegemony works within sport, as well as how dominance is maintained and sometimes challenged or resisted.

More precisely, in this book we aim to use the concept of hegemony as an analytical lens to explain not only power and dominance in diverse sport settings, but also resistance and compliance, stability and change. This enables us to understand the challenges that individuals may face when trying to move outside the dominant line of thinking concerning what is to be expected and idealized, and what is not. To understand power and dominance it is necessary to focus not only on those who are privileged and whose worldview has become the cultural norm, but also those who are disadvantaged or marginalized within the same culture.

In this book, we will use several examples of how hegemony can be used not only as an analytical concept, but also as a way of understanding and deciphering how power forms and operates in both social and cultural structures, as well as in people's daily lives. We will use examples from our own research on anti-doping, on gender, and more to scrutinize how power has formed organized sport as an institution and how that power operates within sport. We will also use secondary literature to further widen our argument and present an in-depth analysis of the mechanisms of hegemony when the analytical lens is directed towards the sport context.

Book Outline

In this first chapter we have presented the main focus of this book and emphasized that hegemony as both concept and theory will be at the heart of our discussion. We have deliberately not centered directly on hegemony in this chapter, but instead provided the context for how and where this concept is most relevant and applicable — as part of analyses of culture and power. In chapter 1 we will present a more comprehensive description of hegemony, the origin of the concept, and how it has been refined over time. This chapter will be primarily theoretical and analytical, whereas the following two chapters (2 and 3) will be more empirically driven and focus on application. In chapter 2 the focus is on gender. We look specifically at how male dominance can be understood and has been addressed in sport. To do so, we use the concept of hegemonic masculinity as the point of departure to discuss the varied ways sports performance, structures, and cultures have historically been imprinted by masculinity, creating two different sets of values and possibilities for men and women in everyday sport. Chapter 2 will address both those who can be described as privileged and those whose perspectives exemplify exceptions to cultural norms. Chapter 3, as the previous chapter, is intended to be empirically driven and serve to show how hegemony as a theoretical frame can be applied for a deepened understanding of sport as an institution. Instead of gender, this chapter will focus on sport governance and policy. We will discuss anti-dopism and how the hegemony of the World Anti-Doping Agency in international sport is both maintained and has come to be challenged. In chapter 4, we discuss the role of theory to understand and analyze power and dominance in sport in general, and the use of hegemony as a theoretical frame in particular. Finally, we present some further readings if you would like to learn more about some of the things we discuss throughout the book. Each chapter ends with questions for further discussion, as below.

Discussion Questions

- Where do we see power and its manifestations in everyday life (government, in universities, friendships)?
- What are examples of productive (soft) and authoritative (hard) power, respectively?
- Where do we find culture?
- How do we change our way of behaving when we move between different cultural contexts (i.e., from lecture to pub)?
- Discuss the relationship between power, domination, and culture in sport.

A link to access additional online resources is provided at: https://doi.org/10.18848/978-1-957792-21-7/CGP

CHAPTER 1

The Concept Of Hegemony: Origin And Developments

In this chapter we will more thoroughly develop and deepen our understanding of the concept of hegemony. We begin by presenting a central scholar in the development of hegemony, Antonio Gramsci, and discuss how he elaborated this concept. We will describe how hegemony was initially developed and used by Gramsci when he picked up the concept. Departing from that discussion, we will then show how the concept and theoretical arguments have further evolved over time. Hegemony has been used within different fields of knowledge, including in the gender debate and within sport governance. These two themes or sites of inquiry (gender and governance) are also the two aspects of hegemony that we will pick up in chapters 3 and 4, respectively. This chapter ends with a short discussion of the relationships between power and resistance and between stability and change, and how power can be exercised through consent rather than brute force.

Antonio Gramsci

In the academic debate on hegemony, one highly relevant scholar is Antonio Francesco Gramsci (1891-1937). He was an Italian philosopher and politician. In his writing, as well as in his political conviction, he was heavily influenced by Marxist theory and ideology. Gramsci was critical of the ways society served to produce differences and inequalities between people through the capitalist system (Fontana 2008). In a similar vein as Karl Marx had argued, Gramsci thought that the capitalist system tended to oppress people in different ways, making them alienated from their own lives by turning them into "human tools" for use in various industries, leading to a repressive society and culture. To challenge this development, in the midst of industrialization, Gramsci founded the communist party in Italy. He took a stand in favor of the labor force (the proletariat, the poor working class) that was dominated by the rich and wealthy (the bourgeoisie). Gramsci aimed to bring about change that would enable individuals to have more say in their life pursuits, rather than being more or less forced to engage in a life run or formed by the principles of Taylorism – life and work organized around machinery and a conveyor belt mentality.

In contemporary western society a critique directed towards the ruling class and its culture would hardly raise too many eyebrows, but in the early years of the twentieth century in Italy, Gramsci's critical ideas and political stance were explosive. In 1926, Gramsci was arrested by the Fascist regime led by Benito Mussolini's government. Consequently, and despite his parliamentary immunity as a politician, Gramsci was taken to prison. It was during this time that he developed not only his famous *Prison Notebooks*, in which he elaborated his theoretical ideas, but also a health condition that eventually led to his death. Due to Gramsci´s imprisonment, his thoughts and ideas were not compiled as a neatly packaged theory or argument. Instead, his collection of around 30 notebooks constitutes a coarse frame of analysis (see: Hoare and Nowell Smith 1999). Despite the slightly fragmented nature of his writing, it was a highly important contribution in twentieth century sociological and political theory.

Cultural Hegemony Of What?

If we set Gramsci´s personal predicaments and political engagement aside, he is perhaps best known academically for his theory
of *cultural hegemony*, which he developed during his incarcer-
ation. He used this concept to describe how capitalism and the
wealthy upper (bourgeoisie) class maintained power over the
lower classes without needing to threaten violence or use coercion. What Gramsci wanted to show was how the bourgeoisie
could dominate through the control of ideas and values – those
things that make up culture. Before we dig more deeply into
Gramsci's theoretical ideas on cultural hegemony, however, it is
important to consider the origins of this concept. Gramsci himself did not invent hegemony, but it was a concept he picked up,
refined, and elaborated on.

The term hegemony derives from the ancient Greek word *he-
gemonia*, which at the time was basically understood as some
form of geopolitical dominance exercised by a state or an empire.
Throughout history there are loads of examples of how states
have exercised their power and achieved hegemony. In the ancient Greece, the politics of Sparta served to form not only war-
riors and military power for Sparta, but also lifestyles and cultural
beliefs that came to form and dominate other Greek city-states for
a period of time. This could be described as the Spartan hegemony, during which a culture that valued heroism and warfare came
to dominate social and cultural life. On another, albeit fictional,
note, in the *Star Wars* movies we see how the evil emperor Darth
Sidious held the whole galaxy under siege through geopolitical
force and the threat of intervention if people did not comply with

the demands of the "dark side." In both cases, we can see how power is exercised with authority and force, but become accepted through culture. Additionally, these examples also demonstrate that such hegemonic power can be contested, challenged, and resisted.

These two examples (Sparta and Star Wars) are general and a bit coarse, and the point here is not to pinpoint the initial meanings or origins of hegemony. Rather, what we want to emphasize is that the concept has evolved and developed over time. Initially it was used to describe how physical, geopolitical force and control were used in societies and this formed and upheld cultures and lifestyles. Later, that line of thinking changed. Gramsci rethought the concept and moved it from its embedded position within discussions on physical oppression and into the terrain of cultural dominance through consent. In this development of the concept, control and power are still central features. Hegemony, then, as Gramsci used it, turned into a sort of cultural monopoly and control.

As Gramsci's writings on hegemony are mainly found in his notebooks, it is difficult to present a clear and final definition of how he understood hegemony. Jackson Lears (1985), however, used excerpts from Gramsci's *Prison Notebooks* to define cultural hegemony as:

> The 'spontaneous' consent given by the great masses of the population to the general direction imposed on social life by the dominant fundamental group; this consent is 'historically' caused by the prestige (and consequent confidence) which the dominant group enjoys because of its position and function in the world of production. (Lears 1985, 568)

At the heart of Lears's description of Gramsci's way of approaching hegemony is the fact that power, control, and dominance over ideas, cultural beliefs, and ideals are to be understood in terms of consent. Power is not necessarily exercised through brute force and authority, and it does not need to be. Instead, power is maintained through dynamic processes in which the oppressed and their oppressors work together to uphold a certain way of life or beliefs about what is valued. Consequently, even in a culturally diverse society we still may have a ruling class (the rich and wealthy) or a ruling gender (masculinity). In this way, these privileged groups have the ability to form and manipulate culture in such a way that their perspectives, aspirations, and general worldview become the taken for granted views and accepted cultural norms and values for the society as a whole. How did Gramsci mean that this worked out then?

According to Gramsci, societies have different values and norms that are expressed and understood as part of the cultural fabric of that very society. But some of these values and norms are viewed as being more correct than others. In a capitalist system, for example, to aspire career success and financial gains may be seen as core values, whereas other aspirations around charity or minimalism are considered less important or even obsolete. It might even be considered "the looser path" in public discourse. Consequently, the formation of a capitalist culture may occur where career, financial strength, and consumption are highly valued and become formative for how that society is organized, and following this how people tend to think about what is normal/right to aspire for. By controlling culture and cultural values, Gramsci suggested that the *status quo* in society could be maintained and legitimized. Put differently, as long as we learn through culture to aspire for certain ideals, other and potentially challenging values will not be as easily recognized or readily pursued – this is the function of hegemony, to set some values as the cultural default.

Through this process of cultural hegemony, a social order that privileges one group over another can be formed.

This line of thinking is also relevant in contemporary capitalist society, where we have a cultural order through which some are able to live privileged lives while others suffer or face barriers to the same type of success. But as the ideas that underpin these privileges are shared by the many, even people who mostly experience the darker sides of capitalist society will routinely still buy into these ideas and cultural beliefs about what constitutes success. For example, the notion of "the American dream" is a strong cultural belief in American society, and though few actually achieve this ideal, the idea of this standard is shared and supported by the many.

A even sharper example of this would be to look at the gendered dimensions of career-making where men and women are taught from an early age to get an education and aim for a well-paid job, only to find out that there is a "glass ceiling" that hinders girls and women from reaching their full potential. Women are still marginalized within many professions and globally they earn less than men, including when they are doing the same work. The reasons for the persistent gender wage gap are of course complex, but surely it is not only the fact that occupations that are associated with femininity usually are less well paid than those associated with masculinity. Cultural beliefs about what constitutes a good leader and a trustworthy and loyal employee are also soaked in gendered understandings that tend to privilege men. Sport and the notion of athleticism, performance, and muscles are no exception from such hegemonic understandings of gender, to which we will return shortly.

What we want to emphasize here is that cultural hegemony is to be understood largely as a question of consent between groups of people. Hegemony works through society and culture. Society is organized around culture – a set of norms, values, and ideals. These ideals provide order in society, even a sense of security and predictability. People will know how to behave and what is expected of them in order to be seen as successful, good, masculine/feminine, etc. But even though dominant culture is shared or accepted by the many, at the same time it can benefit some more than others.

In the remainder of this chapter we will look at how hegemony has been used by more contemporary scholars. The intention here is to use the discussion above as starting point to show how the concept of hegemony can be used within different areas of research. In doing so, we will further develop our understanding of the concept and the analytical gaze that it offers, while at the same time briefly illustrate how it can be applied in different contexts and settings. In chapters 2 and 3 that follow we will work further on the question of application and use of theory when analyzing and explaining empirical data.

From Patriarchy To Hegemonic Masculinity

Just as the meaning of hegemony has evolved over time, so have the concepts used to analyze power and dominance of men over women changed over time. In gender research, for example, one term often used to describe men´s general power over women has been the concept and notion of patriarchy. As noted in the previous chapter, this term describes structural conditions through which men/fathers/masculinity can dominate family life in different ways and allow men to hold privileged positions in society, to the detriment of women. However, this system is neither unchangeable nor unchallengeable. Following this, patriarchy as a concept used to describe the authoritative power men holds over women in general has been called into question, including by the Australian gender scholar and pedagogue Raewyn Connell (1987; 1995).

Connell's groundbreaking study on the transformation of masculinity was published in 1995. This theory, roughly, developed from a growing critique of previous theories on masculinity and family life, in which men's power over women were analyzed mainly in terms of social roles and more or less static gender polarities. Connell suggested that ideas about men as instrumental leaders, for example in sport and family life, and women as subjugated and only having emotional and expressive functions in society, were outdated. Connell was critical towards such functional understandings, in which men and women were seen as having different functions in society and tended to lead to biological determinism. *Biological determinism* is the idea that one's biology (e.g., their sex at birth) controls their characteristics, behaviors, or social position. Instead, Connell wanted to put the focus on relationships and social life, especially the ways power and dominance were upheld in a more dynamic and cooperative way. Here we can see how Connell used the question of consent, which was central in Gramsci's thinking.

Analyzing the relational aspects of gender can, of course, be done in different ways. It can be debated in terms of an informal agreement, in which men and women in a society or culture roughly agree on the tasks, attitudes, behaviors, and more that they associate with men and women, respectively. This informal cultural agreement can be described as a *gender contract*. This is a cultural agreement that stipulates what men are expected to do and be like, and this is understood in contrast to what women are expected to do and be like. Agreement or even awareness of this contract is not necessarily an active decision made by individuals. Often, it is the result of observing, learning, and having behaviors corrected in order to conform with the cultural order.

As a hypothetical illustration of this, if you asked one hundred randomly selected people about what they associate with masculinity and femininity the answers would likely track onto hegemonic gender ideals. Responses could focus things that are considered typical interests, skills, careers, etc. for men and women. There would likely be some outliers, but pictures painted would likely present opposing categories with few overlaps between them. This would then represent a collective understanding or a cultural agreement about what masculinity and femininity look like. This agreement in itself is not necessarily a problem. However, what makes it an issue of power is that the things that tend to be identified as masculine are often considered better and more valuable within society and culture. The gender contract, then, inevitably also brings a certain order to things, what we might call a *gender order*.

Concepts such as patriarchy, gender contract, and gender order provide important theoretical tools that help us build an understanding of men's and women's experiences and roles in contemporary culture and society. The concepts are however largely unable to capture or explain the diversities found within gender. For example, that masculinity and femininity can each be done or performed in many different ways. These variations within gender are also ordered in relation to each other. As such, there are different ways of doing masculinity and femininity, but some ways of doing these are considered more correct than others. To try to explain these complex power relationships between and within genders, Connell introduced the concept of *hegemonic masculinity*.

In 1995, Connell defined hegemonic masculinity as follows:

> Hegemonic masculinity can be defined as the configuration of
> gender practice which embodies the currently accepted answer
> to the problem of the legitimacy of patriarchy, which guarantees
> (or is taken to guarantee) the dominant position of men and the
> subordination of women (Connell 1995, 77).

Hegemonic masculinity is both the prevailing form of masculinity expected within a culture and the mechanism through which
the current gender order is maintained. This is especially true in
societies or subcultures in which the values, ideals, and skills associated with masculinity are set as the cultural default. In many
Western cultures, the hegemonic form of masculinity is closely linked to attributes such as strength, aggression, leadership,
bread-winning, and heterosexuality. As masculinity also tends to
be at the top of the gender order, these traits are the more highly
valued than those associated with other forms of masculinity and
even more highly than those associated with femininity.

Connell stressed the connection between masculinity and power, and how this results in men's dominant position over wom-
en (e.g., patriarchy and gender order). Hegemonic masculinity
is thus tightly connected to patriarchy, and also understood as a
strategy to legitimize a particular gender order. That is, it is a joint
understanding within a culture of what constitutes masculinity
or femininity – including the attributes, expectations, and roles
associated with each gender. The fact that there is a gender order
reveals that these notions of each gender are not value-free. To
further develop this argument, Connell suggested that there are
many masculinities and femininities and that none of these are
neutral in relation to one another. To explain and examine different ways of doing masculinity in relation hegemonic masculinity,
Connell used the concepts or positions of *complicit* and *subordi-*

nate. The complicit position is complex. It is close to the hege-monic position and, as a result, part of the constant negotiation concerning where boundaries are drawn between masculinity and other subordinated gender positions – those associated with fem-ininity and un-manliness.

The reason for using these positions is that there are few people who can embody and sustain the hegemonic position at all times. Despite this difficulty, the hegemonic ideal has the power to de-termine which social and cultural values constitute normative guidelines for other people in their daily life. In reality, most peo-ple have a strained relationship between their own life situation and the effort of achieving or even copying hegemonic patterns of masculinity. The hegemonic ideal still sets the tone for what is expected in terms of gender, but few will constantly conform to that standard.

Following this, and with the help of these different positions, Connell aimed not only to create a theoretical framework to an-alyze how different gender configurations – the various ways of doing gender – within and between gender are related to one an-other, but also to clarify how different practices and situations serve to create a changeable gender order, through a constellation of cultural ideals, institutional power, and politics (Andreasson 2015). One important aspect of this theoretical frame is that the hegemonic position is always contestable. Even though it is the prevailing form, it is still open to challenge and subversion. This is why hegemonic masculinity is to be viewed as a dynamic con-cept that embraces the possibility of transformations in gender relations. Put differently, hegemonic masculinity does not aim to capture static patterns of masculinity, but to capture differenc-es and tensions between them. Obviously, masculinity does not "look" the same in all cultures, contexts, or across history. Rather, masculinity is "done" differently in different cultures. The concept of hegemony is able to capture these differences and flexible enough to allow an examination and understanding of the prevailing form of masculinity within cultural settings.

Additionally, hegemony does not mean the total oppression of women. On the contrary, women may understand hegemonic patterns as natural or normal – what is expected of each gender according to the gender contract. Due to this, there may be, at times, a more or less perfect match or alliance between hegemonic masculinity and *emphasized femininity*. Emphasized femininity refers to the ways some women quite willingly accommodate the interests and desires of men. Emphasized femininity is the contrast to the hegemonically masculine position. Indeed, it may be understood as the prevailing form of accepted or expected femininity. Femininity in this form is demure, domestic, and acquiesces to masculinity. This strategy of conformity to heterosexual norms of attraction, however, stands in stark contrast to different subversive forms of resistance towards hegemonic masculinity.

To briefly summarize, hegemonic masculinity is a dynamic concept that aims to capture how relationships between men and women and within each gender can be understood in relation to power and culture. Hegemonic masculinity operates on two levels. First, it represents a rather sharp image of an idealized masculinity, and this can underpin how individuals form lifestyles and practices. This is on the individual level. Second, on a structural level, it also represents the cultural dynamic that is created through these individual lifestyles. That dynamic tends to give (some, hegemonically masculine) men more power and thereby more benefits (material, cultural, and financial) in society. This cultural dynamic of power thus represents the social processes through which men's gendered practices are seen as superior to women´s in general, and where hegemonic conceptualizations of masculinity serve to subordinate women and marginalized forms of masculinity.

The ways this hegemony is upheld, however, may look different depending on the culture or context in which it plays out. Nevertheless, in many cultural contexts, such as elite sport and gym and fitness culture, men have historically been able to reap social recognition for their efforts and performances, whereas women have been questioned both as athletes and women for similar abilities. In the next section, we will look briefly at the intersection of sport and family life to illustrate how this theoretical frame can be applied to understand daily life. Central here are the solutions families choose to deal with their particular challenges through consent and what feels natural, and what this means in terms of gender dynamics.

Political Hegemony And Governance: Hegemonic Regimes In Sport

Hegemony can also be seen within the political realm, such as in relations between countries. Indeed, there have been numerous attempts within the field of international relations to conceptualize how a single state acting as a stabilizing force can work to foster international cooperation and prevent conflict. Countries, however, are not limited to other countries and governments in their interactions and they often engage with non-governmental actors to address problems or issues (i.e., poverty, disease, effects of climate change, economic deprivation, etc.) affecting one or more countries. Non-governmental organizations (NGOs) such as Médicins sans Frontières (MSF) work with local aid organizations and states to provide medical aid and support. This requires cooperation across organizations, though MSF has become recognized as the global leader in assessing and providing medical support due to their positive reputation and expertise. In many ways, NGOs such as these fill important roles that countries either cannot or could not do as efficiently across borders.

Sport organizations, especially international sports federations and organizations, are no exception. These groups will often cooperate with one another and many share similarities in their structure and function as sport governing bodies. However, international sport governance is complex, as it requires cooperation from a range of sometimes competing stakeholders, from the local to the global levels of sport organizations. Drawing on work from the field of international relations, Jedlicka (2018) argues that we can use the notion of a *regime* to understand sport governance. A regime is a collection of functions and characteristics that guide actions. Regimes include "implicit or explicit principles, norms, rules, and decision-making procedures" (Krasner 1982, 186, cited in Jedlicka 2018). Such a system, then, would rely mostly on adherence to such ideas and processes by member organizations, groups, or even governments.

Hegemony is one way of understanding how such regimes are held together in some circumstances. There has been considerable attention paid to understanding the role of a hegemonic actor in creating stability among a disparate group of stakeholders, especially internationally. Within international relations, this has often considered the role of a leading state (e.g., the United States) that can leverage its power to maintain stability among less powerful states or an organization (e.g., the United Nations) that sets out a system of values and processes for members to follow. Though the US does have the ability to threaten military power or other forms of coercion, generally the hegemon is thought to rely on its ability to lead by example, provide goods, and convince others to follow and uphold its ideals rather than threatening force or violence.

In sport we can see this when considering organizations like the International Olympic Committee (IOC). The IOC has no formal state power, but it has emerged as a moral leader within global sport. Its stated values around fair play, sportsmanship, and excellence – highlighted in grand ceremonies at the Olympic Games – underpin much of what the general public expects from sport. It also brings together disparate sports and stakeholders to work together under its event umbrella, providing an unparalleled platform for many sports and athletes. This is especially true with regard to smaller sports that rely on the Olympics for their interest and survival. In this way, the IOC has become a hegemonic force in world sport and is able to set the tone and expectations for how federations will act to remain involved in the Olympic Movement. This helps ensure some stability across countries and sports, such as rules around minimum age requirements or athlete wellbeing. This does not mean that there is no room for change. Indeed, the IOC has faced some upheaval, including when some of its member organizations and countries lost faith in its ability to carry out anti-doping functions following a series of scandals in the 1980s and 90s. This pressure led to the creation of the World Anti-Doping Agency (WADA) who then eventually became the global hegemon for anti-doping in sport. This is the topic we will return to in chapter 3. Nevertheless, the IOC has retained its hegemonic position within the international sport regime. Through this, the IOCs influences not only countries and organizations but also forms a set of cultural values that athletes around the globe tend to aspire in their efforts to qualify for participation.

Extreme Sport And Family Life: A Short Illustration Of Hegemony And Gendered Patterns

Ironman triathlons – extreme multi-sport races comprised of 3.8km swim, 180.2km bike, and 42.2km run segments – are difficult and time consuming endeavors. The sport itself, like many sports, has been dominated by male participants and governing officials throughout its history. Indeed, most international and some national sport governing bodies remain gender imbalanced in favor of men at executive levels (see: Gaston, Blundell, and Fletcher 2020). Though women tend to have a shorter history as participants, often from their exclusion from taking part in many sports, there are efforts by many sport bodies and organizations, including the IOC, to increase women's representation within sport governance. Increasing women's representation at the governance level can have a positive impact on women's participation (Ibid.).

Ironman triathlons are a sport that has been and remains male dominated: an average of 25% of Ironman participants each year are women (Bridel 2015). Though the name Ironman is often used in a gender inclusive way to refer to race finishers, it does underscore its links with masculinity. Television coverage of Ironman races has also tended to focus on women athletes as wives, mothers, daughters, etc in telling their stories, while men were framed differently (Ibid.). This idea that sport, and especially extreme sport, is really for men is reinforced at the levels of both the governance and participation.

In an article published in 1990 and then reprinted in *The Men and the Boys* (2000), Connell discussed the experiences and thoughts of an Ironman triathlete named Steve Donoghue. This study focused on the difficulties Steve experienced when it came to combining his sport career with his family or personal life. His coach was trying to discourage him from entering into intimate relationships, as he believed this would have a negative impact on Steve´s training. This case study served to illustrate a more general pattern found within sport, concerning combining sport, family life, and work.

Hambrick, Simmons, and Mahoney (2013) have shown that Ironman triathletes face different obstacles in their pursuit of athletic progress, such as time restraints and negotiations regarding their workload within their families. This is discussed in terms of a time-based and strain-based leisure-work-family conflict. Basically, what they are saying is that it is really difficult to make time for both sport and being present and engaged in family life (e.g., taking care of children, doing domestic work, etc.). Research also suggests that this conflict might be most pronounced for women who often cut down considerably on time devoted to athletic activities after marriage, mainly due to traditional and stereotypical gender expectations (Taniguchi and Shupe 2014). Women are thus (culturally) expected to focus on the home and care of children, and sport should only be of secondary interest. Ruseski et al. (2011) have also shown that time spent caring for children have a diminishing effect on sport participation. Seemingly, then, sport participation creates restraints in relation to family life (and vice versa), but these restraints do not affect men and women equally. Clearly, there is a dimension of gender at work here, regarding how such restraints are played out and manifest.

In a research project we undertook some years ago, we interviewed men and women preparing for triathlon competitions in Sweden about how they combined training and family life. Among the participants, usually both partners were involved in the sport, and this impacted other aspects of daily life. One woman described it as follows:

> There is not much free time each day. I guess every quarter of
> an hour is accounted for. So if you have any spare time, then
> you have training. And that wears you down. Makes you ask
> yourself, is it worth it? Am I gonna do this again? So, what is
> disappearing is having spare time, doing nothing. Often when
> my husband is out for something, maybe also training, you have
> to make use of what you have. In the evening he might go and
> train and I might sit in the basement on a wind trainer or some-
> thing, so that one of us is home with the kids. (Emma)

Investing a considerable amount of time on training simply
means that there is less time for domestic work and care for children. This equation is something that was expressed repeatedly
among the participating families in this project. Regarding how to
solve the equation, the participants also talked about their family
lives in terms of trying to solve things mostly equally. As it turned
out, however, when asking the participants to describe how they
practically dealt with the lack of time, another pattern emerged.
Indeed, the women interviewed tended in practice to become the
primary caretakers and homemakers when time strained lifestyles
became too strained, while the men could prioritize their training.
Another participant explained how he and his wife (who also was
involved in the sport) solved things when they became parents:

> When we had our son, Anna cut down considerably on her train-
> ing. She started to travel with me. At this time, I worked active-
> ly on the Triathlon enterprise. I had not competed there, but I
> travelled to Europe for competitions instead. Anna chose to go
> with me, so we have been to many competitions in Europe. She
> stopped doing long distance when our son came. She trained a

little bit, but backed off and stopped competing, and she also gave me the chance to exercise much more. (Joseph)

This pattern, reflecting how sport participation impacted the division of labor within family life, repeated itself in a majority of the interviews conducted for the project. Though they described their family life and training as dynamic and in terms of sharing things equally, some gendered patterns clearly emerged. In these, the men could reap benefits in terms of being freed from household work in order to train for their next competition more often. This also offers a practical example of how social and gendered norms work to uphold hegemonic patterns in sport and in family life.

Central to this brief look at a triathlon project is that the patterns that emerged – the men tending to focus on sport and the women tending to fall back on their athletic pursuits to focus on home and children – is that it is all done through and supported by cultural and gender norms and expectations rather than by force or coercion. Indeed, this is reflected in both the history and the governance of the sport, both of which have male dominated. We will return to the notion of hegemonic masculinity and how Connell's theory can be applied further in the next chapter.

Conceptual Take-Aways

In this chapter we have traced the development of the concept of hegemony. Departing from Gramsci's analysis on hegemony we have moved to consider different ways this concept has been deployed as the basis of theoretical work on two very different topics that we will pick up in the next two chapters: gender and sport governance. Despite the differences in application, there are some common elements of hegemony that are worth highlighting here. First, there is the relationship between power and resistance. Though hegemony suggests that the prevailing view or understanding of power is a certain way, this power is not fixed. Rather, it is always subject to challenge or even resistance. In this way, the hegemon is constantly negotiating its position. This assumes that power and its exercise is dynamic and can change if faced with a strong enough challenge. This is true whether its women challenging the notion of contact sports being men-only or if it is sport federations pushing back against an IOC rule. Though the challenge may be imbalanced in favor of the hegemon, change is possible and power balances can shift.

Another element is how hegemonic power is exercised. Hegemony is rooted in social life and both shapes and is shaped by culture – norms, values, and ideas. This means that hegemony generally does not require force or other coercion. Instead, it relies on cooperation – sometimes unwitting – between groups to reinforce and uphold these patterns. In terms of gender, this may be men and women performing masculinity and femininity in what have become stereotypical ways (e.g., men engage in professional careers, women maintain the domestic sphere), while in international sport governance it may mean that sport federations agree to make rule changes according to agreed upon processes rather than back room deals. In both cases, a level of consent to these norms, values, and processes is required for the hegemonic patterns to persist.

Finally, for this chapter, there is the relationship between stability and change. This builds on the first two elements, as the power of hegemony rooted in a shared culture helps ensure stability. For example, gender inequality has persisted because of the power of gender norms that reinforce this system. However, even where broad patterns are stable there is scope for change, often brought about by challenges to such norms or values. Women entering the workforce and becoming leaders in their own right has challenged male dominance in the professional sphere. While men often remain the privileged group, women have made huge amounts of progress and shifted some beliefs and views about who can have careers and what women are capable of. Ideals, however, are not always reflected in daily life practices. Change is often accompanied by backlash, which can happen in other places, contexts, or arenas. Conversely, stability does not necessarily equal a static status quo. We will pick up on and further examine these elements of hegemony in the next two chapters.

Discussion Questions

- Italian philosopher Antonio Gramsci elaborated hegemony as a concept. Why would understanding hegemony be important for him?
- How can hegemony explain a particular type of power and dominance?
- How does cultural hegemony clarify the relationship between dominance and common consent, even when there are conflicting ideals in subcultural groups?
- Discuss how the concepts of gender contract and gender order are related to hegemony?
- How can hegemonic masculinity help us understand gender in society?
- How can hegemony help us understand the relationship between state and non-state actors?

A link to access additional online resources is provided at: https://doi.org/10.18848/978-1-957792-21-7/CGP

CHAPTER 2

Hegemonic Masculinity And Team Sports

Historically, and by tradition, time spent on strengthening the body and generally engaging in sport performance cultures resonates well with what Mosse (1996) describes as the masculine stereotype. Interestingly, Mosse described this as a stereotype but largely he was referring to a normative and dominating masculine ideal. In his construction of this ideal, Mosse was inspired by militarism from the first and the second world wars, and the idea of the warrior. It is not that easy to follow how Mosse suggested this ideal has developed since the 1750s and onwards, but some classically masculine-associated characteristics are reoccurring, such as a strong character, physical strength, discipline, determination, and a well-built masculine body. Against this ideal, Mosse positioned other masculinities (i.e., homosexuals, hippies, and in general men who aim for an alternative masculinity or body). What Mosse put forth was an argument in which a normative masculinity is defined in relation other masculinities, a position that is also in Connell's theories of gender (1995, see previous chapter).

The historical exposé that Mosse presented was well argued and rich in its presentation. At the same time, Mosse moved between men and bodies as more or less sympathetic in a worrying way. Fascist men and their ideal bodies are merged with socialist ideals and a more general description of normative masculinity in society. If the intention was to describe and analyze a warrior masculinity and a performance oriented male body – such as what might be found in the military or in sport, for example – there is not so much to question here. But as an illustration of a more dominant and hegemonic cultural ideal in society, this study is less convincing. During the 1990s, and onwards, we can also see that the interest in historical analyses of masculinity increased. Several of these studies showed similar tendencies as pointed out by Mosse, but they also emphasize how different masculine ideals can be connected to factors such as social class, arguing that middle class values tend to dominate and form certain masculine ideals in society.

The relationship between sport, as both an institution and a culture, and wider society is complex. This relationship has also been discussed vividly in the scholarly debate. Some scholars have suggested that sport should be understood as a societal mirror. The idea here is that by analyzing sport activities we can gain insights in how things like gender, power, and equality play out not only within the world of sport, but also in society. Studying sport thus gives insights and a deepened understanding of social norms and values. Others, though, have instead put forth the significance of separating contexts and (sub)cultures, suggesting that what happens in sport is not so much a mirror of society but rather a (counter)reaction to it. As some social norms and cultural values serve to discipline and control the individual, sport can facilitate the possibility to explore and develop counter-cultural values or subcultures. Accordingly, sport, recreation and lifestyles sometimes have been understood as free zones where people can relax from the pressure that mainstream society and common culture places on the individual. Clearly, both these perspectives on the relationship between sport and society have arguments in their favor and the debate continues. Here we will settle with the conclusion that there is an ever-present tension and interdependence between what happens in sport and what happens in society, as well as how this relates to individuals' understandings of society. Questions concerning gender are no exception to this.

In this chapter, we discuss how hegemonic conceptualizations of gender may manifest in sport and in relation to surrounding society. The chapter will depart from the concept of *hegemonic masculinity* and *emphasized femininity* (as presented in previous chapter) and our ambition is to illustrate how these concepts and the gender theory presented by Raewyn Connell can be applied when trying to understand how athletes understand their performances and ambitions. The chapter is partly based on our own empirical data that we have gathered over the course of several years, as well as on secondary literature. We will begin with a brief introductory overview of how the gendering of sport has played out in the scholarly debate. This is followed by two sections in which we will look at team sports and gender. First, we look a male handball team, and second a women's football team. We aim to show how the athletes on these two teams talk about performance, gender, and their sport. In doing so, we will actualize Connells conceptual contribution and show how it can be applied to aid our understanding of these men's and women's narratives. The chapter ends with a short summary in which the main takeaways and implications from the chapter are presented.

The Gendering Of Sport

In the scholarly debate, it has been repeatedly shown that gendered norms, although expressed differently in different times and cultures, are reproduced in sport. As such, gendered norms have served to maintain and legitimize an image of men's dominance, power, and precedence in sport and society. Indeed, sport has been understood as a masculinizing process, perhaps even a recipe, through which normative masculine ideals can be achieved or reached. That is, through socialization, boys can learn how to become men (Kidd 2013). Socialization is here understood as a prolonged process through which cultural values and norms are transferred socially and internalized by the individual. Through participation in sport, young boys have thus been taught how to act and react in sport to become successful, "real" athletes, and in doing so also internalized normative conceptions of how one should be to be a so-called real man.

When it comes to women and sport, the picture has been quite the opposite. In public discourses and among sport stakeholders (including athletes themselves), women´s participation was long questioned, if not outright condemned. Historically, women's sport has been considered to be immoral, unhealthy, and even dangerous. In the early twentieth century, for example, medical expertise emphasized the negative effects of women's sport participation. It was thought that sport would make women infertile, and that physical activities could hurt their breasts and complicate their menstrual cycles. In general, it was thought that sport would make women's bodies physically deformed (Hjelm 2004). Later, in the 1950s, these arguments changed and were gradually replaced by more moralistically based judgments deriving from strong (masculine) ideas about what respectable women should and should not do. To perform with stamina, to sweat, or to straddle a saddle, just to mention a few examples, were seen as immoral, unaesthetic, and unfeminine at that time.

Today, one may smile a bit when reading about these uninformed (and false) worries, through which poorly disguised attempts to limit women's participation in sport were made. Just because previous prejudices have been called into question does not mean that they are obsolete in contemporary sport and society, however. Quite the contrary. Norms and cultural ideals concerning competitive sport in the twenty-first century are still often linked to and associated with different notions of men and masculinity. The limiting of women's engagement today may be less explicit and perhaps more sophisticated, but it is still there. Indeed, constructions of masculinity are changing and being rethought, but such transformational processes are often uneven and can vary greatly between different sport and national contexts. Taking one step forward sometimes also includes one step back. Therefore, in certain settings we may find more or less stereotypical masculinities being played out, whereas other settings may embrace a more dynamic and gender-inclusive understanding of sport, gender, and performance (Magrath, Cleland, and Anderson 2020). The gendering of sport and the gender order in sport, then, is a question of both stability and change.

From a situation in which predominantly young men participated in sport, in many places today boys and girls, as well as men and women, can engage in some sort of organized sport or other form of physical activity during childhood, adolescence, or adulthood. While it may not be the case that sport is considered to be an exclusively male domain, men are still, nevertheless, often considered to be better at sport compared to women. This feature of sport culture remains, despite strong efforts and systematic work for gender equality.

Thus, traditional masculine values and a gender order that privileges men prevail in sports culture, despite the division between the genders being more blurred today compared to the situation 50 years ago. This also relates to why men and male sport are usually favored when it comes to allocation of resources and media attention. Sport can be seen as one significant player in the process of maintaining the idea that men's physicality, competitiveness, and assertiveness is natural and superior to women's. This feature of sport culture remains, as do hegemonic conceptualizations of masculinity within sport more than two decades into the 21st century, and despite systematic work for gender equality in sport and society in many countries.

In the sections that follow we will look at how gendered meanings and the effects of hegemonic masculinity play out in some athletes' daily lives.

A Real Athlete And Others: Men In Team Sport

In this section, we will focus on a study in which one of us, Jesper, conducted a longitudinal ethnographic study of a Swedish handball team (Andreasson 2007). The team members were not elite athletes, but still fairly serious about their sporting performances and aiming to proceed up through the sport's divisions. Jesper, who previously had played handball, decided to join the team to study how gender and, more specifically, how masculinity was understood and constructed among the team members in their everyday lives. Following this, Jesper participated in training, played in matches, and went to training camps with the other members of team. He spent four years as a member of the team. The men on the team knew he was conducting a study of their team, which they were reminded of from time to time when interviews were conducted. In the study, he paid attention to how team members talked about their own performances and what they wanted to achieve as sportsmen. He also tried to discuss their understandings of a successful athlete in more general terms, as well as their understanding of muscles and masculinity, among other things.

The prolonged study on the men's team contained different approaches to everyday life in team sports. One part of the study concerned cultural ideals and how the notion of athleticism was understood among the men. Another part concerned looker room talk and how the men discussed gender issues in seclusion from outsiders. Regarding the official, and public, narrative of what constitutes an athlete, the men, perhaps unsurprisingly, were rather uniform in their perspective concerning how to act and what to pursue in order to be successful and to be recognized by other team members. Some cultural ideals were repeatedly put forth as worth striving for within the group, such as being prepared to unconditionally sacrifice one's physical self for the team, which usually meant being prepared for physical collisions and hits without backing down. The ability to develop and nurture both physical and mental toughness was repeatedly underscored by the men. It was through this sense of collective toughness that the men aimed to dominate their opponents. Further, the men put forward an instrumental approach to the body, where fears of clashes against opponents, pain, and other feelings were suppressed during a match. The players described this instrumentality as a central component in their staging, or doing, of athleticism. These cultural ideals (collectiveness, instrumentality, emotional numbness, and physical domination through the hard and muscular body) were described as follows by one of the team members:

> You have to be physically prepared for what you are doing, which means that you have to be trained for it. You have to have a good physique. A handball player is supposed to be fully devoted to what he aims to do. He should know what to do, evaluate what he has done, and always push the limits. You gotta push your own limits. And the best way to do that if you are not able to do it for yourself is to surround yourself with those who have that mentality. You give it your best and the bar should always

> be moved upwards, just another five centimeters. You have to
> bring that extra to it when it hurts.

Operating in a group, being inspired by other men, and pushing the limits are seen here as central components when explaining what constitutes an authentic team player and athlete. Another man continued and talked about motivation and inspiration:

> When you look at Per in the defense, I mean when he literally
> knocks down this giant man among the opponents, you get re-
> ally motivated yourself. *Dammit, I'm gonna give them hell*, like
> that. Then there are those who are pushing you, urging you to
> go on even if you are tired. Then, the only thing to do is to keep
> going, and there is someone who shows the direction.

The cultural narrative about the performing athlete prepared to inflict pain on others and weaponize the body through collective aspirations is all too familiar and is a bit of an echo from sport studies conducted over decades (Messner 1990; Andreasson and Johansson 2019a). However, just as often as these ideals are expressed, they are also contrasted with notions of femininity and what is perceived as fragile and weak. The ability to perform as a unit, to be in control of one's emotions, and being able to push through a solid defense are clearly understood as masculine traits. This is exemplified in these interview excerpts:

> I mean, women are more about emotions and such. They are
> more like that, I think. Men are rougher. I dunno. The physical,
> that sort of thing. Girls are more into impressions, feelings, and
> that sort of thing. Maybe they use their senses in a completely
> different capacity.

> We are boys. I mean, dammit if there were a feminine style
> in the team. Then we would play ladies handball. I mean, it's
> tougher. We are tougher towards each other and have a tougher
> way of communicating. With ladies there is more talk behind
> the back and that sort of thing. We are more straightforward in
> our communication. *You are a fuckhead, I don't like you, but
> now we are in the same team so let's focus on that.*

Another man continued:

> Female, I mean just hearing that word doesn't make me think
> about sport. Even now, when we talk about handball all the
> time and when we say femininity, then I think about the ladies
> handball team, because we are not feminine. And then if you
> continue that line of though I guess I can conclude that those
> women playing there, in the ladies team of our club....that is not
> femininity for me anyway.

What we see here is how certain cultural ideals and ideas of the
performing athlete are soaked in traits that are associated with
masculinity. Acting like a "real" athlete is also acting like a quite
stereotypical man. As such, a real athlete is not a woman. What
we can see emerging here is a rather rigid gender order. But there
is more to it. Here we begin to see a discussion on differences
within gender emerging. In the previous quotes, the women handball players were not viewed as feminine, which can be interpreted as an expression that women handball players do not meet the
criteria for *emphasized femininity*. In a similar vein, there were
also men on the handball team who was considered to be unable
to live up to the masculine standard. One player said the following about another:

> Nah, but I guess Joel is bit of an outsider. Why is he that? Yeah,
> maybe he is just unlucky and sort of mum's little boy. Nah, I
> dunno, but the group sets an ideal you know. The group sets an
> idea, a standard, regarding how to be. It may be stupid, but that
> is how it is. The group is rather quick in condemning people and
> I don't think there is a way around that.

Joel's outsider status noted above is explained in terms of him being bit of a mama's boy, that is unable to live up to the standards
and cultural ideals of the collective. Another man continued on
this topic:

> You cannot be a mama's boy when entering the pitch, nor sits
> down in the locker room. You can't be this mother-in-law's
> dream, like granny and grandpa just loves to spoil. Nah, you
> have to toughen up, become rougher, coarser when playing
> handball.

This emerging narrative from the team constructs masculinity as
superior to femininity. We can also see how differentiations within gender manifest in the narratives. Women playing handball are
seen as atypical women, or they are not associated with femininity, while men that cannot live up to the ideals of the collective
are seen as outsiders and juvenile (mama's boys). This narrative
and logic was also present when the men described how they in-
teracted in the locker room. Whereas the notion of the athlete was
largely a public construction that was presented and performed
under the gaze of an audience, the locker room was an exclusive
space were the men could expand their repertoire. In this seclud-
ed space, the men sometimes amused themselves by making fun
of women and portraying them as passive and sexualized objects

that they placed below themselves in an imaginary gender order. In a similar way, the derogatory term "fag" was used as an
imaginary figure that allowed the men to express and show that
they are a group where heterosexuality is obligatory. These two
figures, the woman and the "fag," were used as symbolic carica-
tures, as anti-identities from whom the men verbally and practically distanced themselves, further highlighting which forms of
masculinity were valued or even accepted within the collective.
Consequently, some masculinities were considered good, while
other masculinities and femininity in general were not.

One team member talked about the locker room mentality and
the expressions of what could be described as a toxic masculinity,
and how the social rhythm in the locker room could be understood in relation to what took place in the men´s everyday lives
outside the sport context:

> Like the media and everything, they really embrace feminism,
> and feel sorry for women and all that. But they rarely look at the
> man. I mean, boys growing up now need to be given an opportu-
> nity to show off a bit. I mean we, boys, have this aggressiveness
> and we need to learn how to deal with that in the best way pos-
> sible. So, sometimes I think that this, what we have here in the
> team, is the little society of boys, were one can be a boy and act
> as such. Then you can go home to your wife and take care of the
> dishes and be gender equal.

Several of the men expressed that they do not have to negotiate
their masculinity when being with their teammates. Everyday
life outside the sport context means a pluralization of voices and
ideals on how to act and behave. Outside the sport context, hegemonic masculinity would certainly constitute a more gender
equal and inclusive masculinity, perhaps even a more feminist

view of sport and society. In daily life these men must negotiate their masculinity in relation to women and other men, which
results in a more dynamic and reflexive masculinity. Within the
team, however, this reflexivity is not called upon. Instead, they
can form their own world where a more domineering masculinity
can be expressed, at the expense of women.

> The view on women is terrible in the locker room. It's probably
> not the actual view that you have. Rather you kind of develop
> it a little bit, so to speak. It's like look at that woman, I could
> do her, just up with the pussy. Yes, but it's just like that. So, the
> view on women is no good. Yeah, she's really horny that one,
> dammit. That's the way we talk about it.

The *free zone* of the male collective is also repeatedly put in contrast with worries about social developments and the notion of the
gender equal man. However, the men's portrayal of the woman
and the "fag" – those that are undesirable – also constituted a
number of limitations for themselves. When they made use of
an aggressive, violent, muscular, and sexist masculinity as a cultural icon for the group, they also excluded not only women and
homosexuals from this collective, but also parts of themselves
that may have been associated with these symbolic figures. For
example, the men found it difficult to display or express certain
aspects of their emotional range. It was as if they were ashamed
of showing affection and care for other men, and therefore felt
forced to imitate what Burstyn (1999) has termed a *violent hy-
per-masculinity* to avoid being called queer. This exaggerated
masculine ideal allows this group of men to show toughness and
controlled aggression in a game situation or to joke disparagingly
about homosexuals and women in the locker room in a seemingly unproblematic way. On the other hand, to tell a teammate

that his friendship was important, to discuss personal relationships, or express concern about the appearance of your body was incompatible with the type of culture and masculinity that was idealized within the team. In this particular sphere, such displays of emotion were largely associated with the feminine, which was profoundly undesirable and therefore difficult for the men to handle or express.

This section has shown how the male handball players' understandings of athleticism and sport were wrapped up in hegemonic notions of masculinity. The official narrative about a strong, performance-oriented athlete is also a narrative about and justification for masculinity. The study also showed how a normative and traditional masculinity can be developed and exaggerated "back stage," in the locker room, which throws a broader commitment to gender equality in society into question. Therefore, it may well be the case that gender equality has increased over time in sports in terms of participation, much to the benefit of girls and women and LGBTQi people (Anderson 2002; 2009), as well as boys and men who do not favor the norms of hegemonic masculinity. However, though some aspects of the situation have improved, many things remain relatively unchanged. It remains a fact that vulgar expressions of masculinity, such as overt sexism and homophobia, keep showing up in sport contexts, particularly homosocial (i.e., male exclusive) ones.

Fighting On And Off The Pitch: Women In Team Sport

Within the same project in which the men in the handball team were followed over time, Jesper also conducted a study on a women's elite football team. This study also used an ethnograph-

ic methodology, consisting of individual interviews, group interviews, observations, and audio recordings from the locker room,
among other things. What soon became clear was that the social
construction of athleticism – that is, how the women talked about
being athletes and what to strive for as athletes – did not particularly differ from how the men on the handball team talked about
sport and performance. As football players, the women wanted to
be physically larger, stronger, and faster than their opponents. On
a psychological level, they wanted to become self-assured, tough,
gain a sense of total commitment to the cause, be part of the team,
and win their games. Below one woman described this view:

> We do not sit on our ass and file our nails. You cannot be like
> that, I mean in football you have to give all you got. Fitness for
> example is important. I can manage to keep the energy level for
> a whole match. I have the energy to go on and on. I can grind
> down my opponent. My strength is that I can keep on going,
> and grind on, all the time. Then there might be someone who is
> really explosive, really fast and someone might push the others.
> You need different types within the team. Someone is strong in
> close combat, that sort of player, and someone is strong within
> the penalty area, I mean nod game.

Another woman continued:

> What I think is really important, is that you shouldn't show
> fear when engaging in close contact with your opponent. If
> I'm about to hit another person in close combat, someone who
> might be 20 centimeters longer than me, and I think that I will
> lose the battle because she is taller than me, yeah, then I have
> lost the battle before it started. I'm quite small so I can't show
> fear in close combat. The most important thing is to have cour-

age. Then there are other physical capabilities as speed and such. But to have the courage and master your fear is the most important thing mentally and speed and strength when it comes to the physical part of the sport.

What we see here is how certain cultural ideals are brought to the fore. In the descriptions of a successful athlete, the women talk about the significance of mastering your fear, of being prepared for physical clashes and battle, and to have enough speed, strength, and courage to defeat opponents. Interestingly, the women also often associated these qualities with masculinity. As an athlete you do not sit and file your nails – a passive activity really only associated with femininity – you are active and performance oriented. This view was expressed or explained in different capacities. For example, in a conversation with one of the players, Jesper and the player began to talk about daily life outside elite sport, and the mentality and culture among the other women in the team. The woman started to talk about how she prepared herself for training and matches. When talking about herself gearing up for football, it was almost as if she suggested that her body started to move in a different way. She explained that outside the sport context she looked at herself as any ordinary woman, but when she put on her shin protectors and laced her football shoes her walk and movements changed: there was one way of performing on the pitch and another when off. In a later interview, she was asked to develop her line of reasoning regarding that feeling and what it meant. Clearly, there were gendered understandings involved in this discussion:

> Yeah, I remember. I think you can see the difference if you would look at us wearing our usual clothing, and then when we are geared up in our training outfits. I think there is a difference,

> in style and how you walk and move around. I mean it's mostly
> on the pitch. It's not in my ordinary life. As for now, when I'm
> not dressed for football I don't think anyone would see it on my
> style. But when you have your training gears and you enter the
> field, you become different. You walk a bit different.

Spending time with teammates and playing football is here understood as not only an identity forming practice, but also a highly embodied (and gendered) experience. It is almost as if engaging in sport has meant that this athlete has develop new bodily
competencies. In a way, what is touched upon here is sort of a
hegemonic narrative in which cultural ideals are saluted, which
means that the people involved in this practice also develop a
way of talking and moving around. That this type of physicality
is associated with masculinity becomes abundantly clear below:

> Yeah, I mean, what I think is feminine is to be charming, cute,
> careful and, yeah, maybe not so powerful. It sounds really neg-
> ative, but it is, if you compare with men. I mean if you look at
> a game or another tough sport, it's a tough surface. It's about
> bringing the toughness to the fore. I don't think it is something
> you can….it's hard to explain. It feels like, when I think of it,
> now when we talk about it, that is how I think about it. So, I
> think football and a football field.

From this we can see how cultural ideals and ideas about successful and tough athletes have been "downloaded" in the locker
room, through the football shoes, and on the pitch. So, in describing a complex identity project and constructing athleticism, the
cultural narrative of being a woman and a football player seemingly does not totally fit together.

Along with the proclivity to describe themselves as tomboys

and make comments to the effect of "I'm probably not like other girls," the women constructed an ideal female football masculinity for the collective (c.f., Halberstam 1998). They argued that this female masculinity has taught them to internalize important traits such as going for it on the football pitch and having things their way. Besides improving their physical prowess, their continual eagerness to become better at running, dribbling, and shooting has also resulted in a sense of mental freedom. This sense is constituted primarily by the transference of the women's trust from the ability of their physical bodies to their self-esteem. This is hardly surprising since athletic skill is judged primarily on physical practice. That the feeling of mental freedom is constructed as a masculine characteristic also became apparent when the women contrasted their own independence with the situation of other women, who were sometimes described as passive, careful, cute, and dependent. By distancing themselves from what they assume are traditional feminine characteristics – emphasized femininity – they constructed a social collective that is perceived as serious, independent, and genuine. In other words, they are a group of real athletes who are therefore implicitly masculine, at least in part.

For the women, playing football has brought both bodily possibilities and limitations. On the one hand, the intensive training regime has given them the opportunity to experience bodily value and a sense of pride in the physical capacity they have developed, an empowered female masculinity. On the other hand, the physical prowess they have earned through hard work sometimes prevents them from viewing their bodies and themselves as normatively feminine, unable to meet the standards of emphasized femininity. As athletes, the women want to become stronger, faster and better. Unfortunately, from the perspective of gender identity, this means that they also have to navigate that such performances may be understood as challenging dominant conceptions

of what men and women are supposed to be like, and thus facing
social stigma. As has been well documented, women's achieve-
ments in the sphere of sport and performance historically have
been met by critique and viewed as an abnormality, mainly due to
narrowly defined gendered scripts (McGrath and Chananie-Hill
2009; Hargreaves 2000). In this way, hegemonic understandings
of gender – and especially of the link between masculinity and
sport – are both challenged and reinforced within women's sport.

Take-Aways: Gender Ideology And Hegemonic Masculinity In Team Sports

This chapter has illustrated how athletes, both men and women,
conform to and reinforce cultural ideals and notions of what is
considered normal or desirable within sports. In doing so, men
and women are upholding and reproducing the unequal standards
that rule the gendered practices common in sport. In the narratives expressing sport values, ideals, and identities, both groups
are consenting to the relationship between athleticism and gender. In order to live up to the identity pretensions that organize
their team sport reality, the athletes moderate certain qualities and
aspects of self (i.e., feminine) while presenting others as central
(i.e., masculine). However, behaviors that select, organize, and
connect different elements of a sporting lifestyle and culture cannot be understood merely as a passive adaptation to hegemonic
masculinity. That a member of a collective complies with a hegemonic definition of reality (the gender of sport culture) does
not mean that the individual is completely in the hands of the
collective or controlled by social structures. The individual generally has the option of choosing and negotiating between doing
one thing instead of the other. Further, there is an intricate balance

between reproducing gendered meanings and questioning them, or between stability and change.

It is important to clarify that the men on the handball team do not exclusively stage themselves as tough and heterosexual men, and the women on the football team are not confined to renegotiating their femininity when their female qualities are in doubt, as a consequence of their more masculine associated performances and constructions of athleticism. The men's way of portraying women in the locker room is sometimes claimed to not be the actual view of women, but rather something produced temporarily in the current athletic context. And the women on the football team sometimes explicitly resist and make fun of male athletes and football teams, describing them as being raised with a "silver spoon" and not preparing for life after elite sport. On those occasions they are trying to use humor and sarcasm to distance themselves from their personal circumstances and sport culture. These examples of oppositional identification are tied to a changeable gender order that the men and the women feel has made significant progress through, for instance, the presence of more women in the professional world, paternity leave, a feminist presence within political parties, and so on. Sport and society do not exists separately from one another, but are inextricably linked and reflecting and shaping one another.

The men and women's practices and ways of reasoning regarding sport culture and gender can be interpreted in different ways. On the one hand, they support and normalize a performance-oriented masculinity within team sports, while at the same time marginalizing other masculinities and demeaning women, femininity, and the female body. Ultimately, this leads to the reconstruction of a social system where men and typically masculine structures are allowed to dominate and rule, and, through their advantageous position, use or exploit women and their possibility to realize their dreams and goals in life, in this case those related to team sports. On the other hand, besides their gender preserving practices, the men and the women have taken notice of and ongoing gender equality debate in public discourse, in sport, and in relation to domestic life. Still, even though the men and the women in each collective knows better or even disagrees with some of what goes on privately or outside the sport context, the power of the hegemonically gendered narratives is great. It is seemingly so powerful that they often simply conform to or ignore or tacitly accept the social rhythm of team sports, rather than offer a serious or radical challenge. Although hegemonic masculinity may at times be questioned to some extent, largely in the realm of team sports certain expressions of masculinity are reproduced and given a culturally privileged position.

Discussion Questions

- What implications does hegemonic masculinity have for women in sport? What are the implications for men?
- What were the core cultural values of athleticism described by the two teams and how do they relate to gender?
- How can masculinity and femininity be enacted in different ways? How and to what extent are each of these valued?
- What are some strategies that could begin to change the dominance of men and masculinity within sport?

A link to access additional online resources is provided at: https://doi.org/10.18848/978-1-957792-21-7/CGP

CHAPTER 3

Sport Governance And The Hegemony Of WADA

As both a concept and theory, hegemony provides the ability to analyze how power and cultural values work among groups or teams of individuals in sport. Hegemony can also be useful for helping us see how institutions, organizations, and even countries can manifest ideas and values through intellectual and/or moral leadership, even outside any national government or policy framework. Many non-governmental organizations (NGOs) working for causes such as human rights, the environment, or global health, have been able to direct values and approaches to social issues that become widely accepted. For example, human rights focused organizations have been successful in defining and then highlighting the importance of human rights. Organizations like Amnesty International or Human Rights Watch have become regarded as global experts on these issues and their voices and views on many issues have become mainstream. This broad acceptance allows them to have a high level of influence on policymakers and other organizations, despite lacking their own power to make or change laws or other decisions directly. From this, these organizations have then been able to identify various rights abuses around the world and pressure countries to make policy changes that conform to their views and recommendations on human rights. Put differently, they have gained a position of power

from which they can control or steer discussions on certain topics, setting certain standards around norms and values within the
debate.

Sport institutions are no exception and one area where we can
apply this line of reasoning and the concept of hegemony is to
the anti-doping system in sport. Since its founding in 1999, the
World Anti-Doping Agency (WADA) has been the global leader
in setting anti-doping policy in sport. WADA does this through its
policy documents, including the World Anti-Doping Code (from
here: the Code) and its supplementary policy documents. These
policies apply to all signatories to the Code, which include international sport federations, professional leagues, and event organizers. As the main and most visible anti-doping organization
and largely responsible for setting the global anti-doping agenda
and approach, WADA holds a hegemonic position in world sport.
They dominate the anti-doping debate and how doping is perceived and handled globally. Of course, maintaining this hegemony requires cooperation and consent from key sport stakeholders, including athletes, sport organizations and governing bodies,
fans, the media, and even countries.

Rather than relying on threats of force (e.g., via the military) for
support for its system and policies, as a non-governmental organization WADA relies on cooperation, consent, and compliance
from sport organizations and national governments. By signing
on to the Code, states and sport organizations have empowered
WADA to create anti-doping policies that they, in turn, consent
to abide by and implement anti-doping policies. This consent has
allowed WADA to emerge as the clear global leader on anti-doping, working in cooperation with national anti-doping agencies
(NADOs) and sport federations. In this position, WADA's agenda
and approach have become broadly accepted as the norm in sport.

That is not to say that WADA and its members avoid using direct power or punishment for infractions. Anti-doping is closely associated with assigning often lengthy competition bans to those who violate anti-doping rules. However, these direct sanctions are targeted at the level of the individual and most commonly at the athletes themselves. We are focused here on how hegemony operates on a more macro level, in the relationships between (inter)national sport governing bodies and member countries.

This chapter will look at how WADA achieved and maintains its hegemony. As in the previous chapter, we will draw on our own research and empirical data to show both how hegemony functions in sport governance and to provide an example of how the concept of hegemony can help us analyze the complex power dynamics around anti-doping policy. We will focus on the relationships and dynamics that underpin and reinforce WADA's hegemony, then we will use the case of the United States' Rodchenkov Act to illustrate what resistance to WADA's position from a national government and national anti-doping agency looks like (Henning and Andreasson 2022). The Rodchenkov Act is a U.S. federal law passed in 2020 that criminalizes doping conspirators at international sports events where any U.S. interests (U.S. athletes, sponsors, organizers, etc) are represented, including those outside the U.S.'s territory.

Anti-Dopism:
The Currently Accepted Answer To Doping

Historically, doping has been understood and perceived in different ways. In the early years of the twentieth century, various substances were used to combat fatigue, increase stamina among soldiers, and aid in sport performance. This was largely done in a non-judgmental fashion, particularly if we compare earlier views with contemporary perspectives on doping. Steroids were also used among Soviet weightlifters and American bodybuilders, among others, as early as the 1950s (Dimeo 2007). A will to experiment and the curiosity of what could be achieved with the help of steroids was central to their development and, at least to some extent, doping was understood as part of a medical and scientific approach to the performing, muscular, and skilled (male) body (Andreasson and Johansson 2019b). The debates shifted around 1957, when the American Medical Association raised concerns about amphetamine use in sport and society. According to Dimeo (2007) this was the birth of the anti-doping movement, which then gradually developed into WADA.

Since it was established, WADA has been very successful at authoring and disseminating the dominant cultural narrative around doping in sport, and largely in society. In essence, it has asserted that doping is incompatible with sport values and that doping must be eliminated from sport. This narrative sets "clean" or doping-free sport as its goal and indicates that the way to achieve this is through a punitive system of prohibiting substances, detecting use of those substances, and then heavily sanctioning athletes for rules violations. These can include returning a positive anti-doping test, failing to comply with the testing procedures, failing to report whereabouts even outside competitive season, among others. The sport sociologist Bernat Lopez (2014) refers to this underpinning ideology as *anti-dopism*. Anti-dopism is:

> ...the ideology or the articulated set of beliefs, principles, dogmas, discourses and slogans sustaining and legitimating anti-doping, which is understood as the ensemble of institutions, personnel, regulations and practices aimed at eradicating doping from sport. (Lopez 2014, 214)

Anti-dopism has become uncritically normalized in both sport and wider society, partly through the dissemination of fear- and health-based messages about the risks of doping. These messages have been supplemented with moral arguments against doping, often linking doped (impure, artificial, or unnatural) bodies with immorality. WADA has institutionalized this moral view of doping, justified by the need to protect the "spirit of sport" – a vague concept derived from the Olympic values of purity and authenticity. Via this cultural narrative, WADA has a gained hegemonic position within global sport.

Linking doping with cheating and immorality also helps justify WADA's approach to anti-doping and the system of athlete surveillance that it relies on. Indeed, athletes are required to provide a urine sample when requested and refusal can result in an anti-doping rule violation. This notion that athletes are inherently suspicious and that refusal to provide a sample – which includes an invasive process of exposing oneself and urinating in front of the sample collector – indicates guilt, clearly reflects the idea that morality can only be upheld by ensuring athletes are complying with anti-doping prohibitions and that this is more important than athlete privacy. Some athletes are also required to provide anti-doping agencies with information about where they will be every day and provide a one-hour time slot during which they must make themselves available for testing at a specified location. This "whereabouts" information is designed to allow testers access to athletes at any time, a level of surveillance that greatly exceeds what non-athletes would expect in the absence of having been found guilty of committing a criminal offence. Athletes' freedom of movement is restricted during their testing time slot, meaning their ability to change plans is limited due to anti-doping's stated need to know where athletes will be at all times.

That athletes must comply with the anti-doping system and

policy requirements in order to participate in sport leaves little opportunity for resistance, as this type of surveillance set out by WADA has been accepted as the necessary condition for "clean sport." Like the "spirit of sport," "clean sport" is a vague but morally charged term. In a sense, its vagueness – are athletes who never test positive for a prohibited substance "clean" even if they have doped? – makes it a powerful tool in support of WADA's agenda. For sport to be "clean" athletes must also be "clean." The alternative, of course, is "dirty sport" or a "dirty athlete" – both of which indicate a sense of moral impurity. The lack of clear definitions for either "clean" or "dirty" means that athletes can be easily categorized without needing to meet clear criteria. For example, an athlete who requires a therapeutic use exemption (TUE) to use a prohibited substance for a medically necessary reason may be labeled a "dirty" athlete, despite the TUE process being the correct method for avoiding an anti-doping rule violation. This situation played out following the 2016 release of athletes' private anti-doping information by the group known as Fancy Bears that showed some high profile athletes had been granted TUEs. Notions of "clean" and "dirty" have become so engrained in sport that athletes who had received TUEs were called into question, despite having followed WADA's own rules. This also highlights how the media serves to both disseminate and reinforce anti-dopism, including aiding in the stigmatization of athletes who step outside the lines, even if done so involuntarily. This can have negative repercussions for athletes, who may be unable to escape the association with doping, immorality, and cheating, despite the circumstances in which the violation occurred. Anti-doping controls, though technically applicable to all levels of organized member sports, are strongest among elite level athletes who are subject to the most surveillance and testing.

These systems of surveillance and moralistic messaging underpin the global anti-doping system. Using these, WADA has created the conditions that force compliance with its agenda, as any challenge can immediately lead to allegations that the challenging party is against "clean" sport, morally corrupt or are potentially "dirty." WADA's hegemonic position within sport is reinforced with each new signatory to its Code, media coverage of successfully catching doping athletes, or athlete speaking in favor of the anti-doping system, among other things. Taken together, all this has set a global expectation for doping-free sport and that the way to accomplish it is through WADA's core prohibit-test-punish approach. The point here is that though WADA does have some authoritative power over athletes, as an organization its hegemonic position is based in its ability to formulate and reinforce through policy the dominating anti-doping narrative – hegemonic anti-doping. Their approach to doping sets the agenda for sport, to which other organizations give their acceptance and consent. In the next section, we consider how the system of anti-doping actors, led by WADA, works to reinforce hegemonic anti-doping.

The Anti-Doping Hierarchy

WADA is the leader on anti-doping, but it does not maintain this position or carry out its agenda on its own and this position is never fully secure. WADA relies on a web of stakeholders for support, including financial. NADOs and national and international sport federations work together to implement and enforce policies and support other anti-doping messaging. National governments have a role, too. Contributions from national governments are the source of 50% of WADA's operational funding, with the other half coming from the International Olympic Committee. Countries have also signed onto the UNESCO International Convention on Doping in Sport in support of WADA's anti-doping approach. Due to the broad acceptance of its position and the importance of anti-doping, WADA enjoys a privileged position that can work in its favor when seeking cooperation and compliance of states. WADA, however, is not a state and must use other means to retain its dominant (hegemonic) position.

Countries have powers that exceed those available to non-state actors, including the ability to make binding laws that supersede rules or policies set by NGOs. They also have powers of police and military, and access to national civil and criminal court systems. Countries may work with NGOs to achieve mutual goals but are under no obligation to do so. As a public-private non-governmental organization, WADA lacks the powers traditionally reserved for governments. It has no authority to make or change policy outside of sport and it does not have its own police force or judiciary. WADA cannot force or prevent countries from making anti-doping laws, but some countries have taken additional policy steps in support of anti-doping by passing national laws regulating doping, including use, purchase, and/or sale of certain substances. When WADA's rules clash with those of a national government, WADA's rules only take precedence within the sport context. For example, a substance that is not allowed under anti-doping rules (i.e., cocaine metabolites) but is legally available for use or consumption in some countries (i.e., coca leaf tea) will still be off limits to athletes.

NADOs are key for enacting WADA's policies and programs but are embedded within national frameworks. This means their status and scope can vary by country, as can the level of resource available to carry out its functions. NADOs are often "closer" to both sports federations and athletes, meaning they are more likely to have local knowledge of specific challenges for anti-doping and opportunities for improving the system. Despite WADA's reliance on NADOs, NADOs do not share an equal footing with WADA in terms of influence or power in policymaking. In a truly cooperative effort, WADA and NADOs would work together to exchange information and ideas to then shape and refine policy based on a balance between WADA's agenda and the realities faced by NADOs. Instead, there appears to be a hierarchy to the anti-doping system with WADA at the top and NADOs at the bottom, with many NADOs feeling powerless and overlooked yet forced to comply with WADA's dictates (Zubizarreta and Demeslay 2021).

Compliance by organizational and government stakeholders, as well as that of athletes, is at the foundation of WADA's hegemonic position, as these are the actors necessary to carry out its policy agenda. Though it cannot use the threat of force to ensure compliance, WADA does have other tools at its disposal. Indeed, WADA's main source of leverage is in its ability to determine compliance with its Code. Athletes from countries found to be non-compliant may be prevented from competing internationally. Of course, athletes who do not comply with the Code by committing anti-doping rule violations also face sanctions in the form of competition bans.

By analyzing how WADA uses socio-cultural beliefs and values to further its agenda, we can see how it wields its power so effectively and maintains a stable hold over anti-doping generally and, as we look at in the next section, over athletes in particular.

Compliance:
Global Policy And The Protection Of Sport

Sport policies seek to codify accepted sport values by regulating athlete behavior, with those found in violation excluded from participation. We see this in numerous ways across sports, especially with regard to fair play and protecting athletes from unnecessary harm. For example, many sport governing bodies seek to protect athletes from injury by regulating contact, which is policed by officials who can call fouls for aggressive or violent behavior and sanctioned through various penalties. By trying to mandate values around substance use, WADA is reflecting a broader pattern of prohibitive drug policies often referred to as the "war on drugs." Such policies are usually focused on recreational substances or substances of abuse and tend to target individuals and carry harsh penalties in the belief that it will force compliance. These "war on drugs" policies have been critiqued as largely ineffective and socially destructive. Yet, the power of the narratives around safety and violence associated with substance use outweigh facts and alternative views or approaches. The hegemonic beliefs about drugs being morally wrong and people who use drugs requiring harsh punishment have bled into sport. Indeed, the language around both types of substance use – recreational and enhancing – is similar. "Getting clean" is often used to indicate ceasing recreational drug use, in a similar way that "clean" athletes ostensibly do not use performance enhancing drugs. As such, WADA and anti-doping advocates were able to seize on a powerful hegemonic narrative and, with a few adjustments, deploy it for their own purposes. Beliefs and ideologies are so strong that WADA is able to force compliance with its agenda among stakeholders who fear backlash if they challenge the mainstream view of anti-doping.

The main source of compliance required by WADA to maintain its position is that from athletes. Athletes are the key stakeholder group affected by anti-doping policies, as much of the system is targeted at athletes and policing their behavior. They are the ones who are surveilled, tested, and required to reaffirm their "clean" status anytime they are asked to do so. Yet, athletes have very little say in any aspect of the anti-doping process. Their inclusion is not voluntary but is compulsory as members of signatory sports federations or leagues. Even minor challenges to anti-doping policies or procedures that may be invasive or extreme can lead to an athlete's morality being called into question, despite their compliance. This requires no action on the part of anti-doping agencies, as their peers, fans, and the media usually police dissenters. The power of the anti-doping narrative is such that there is very little, if any, room for dissent. Any perceived reluctance or challenge to the "war on doping" may result in the offending athlete becoming stigmatized – being indelibly marked as bad or shameful. This may require athletes who do have legitimate grievances with the system to remain silent to avoid stigmatizing accusations of being a doper or of being sympathetic to them. In short, to be an athlete in sport – at least at the levels where testing is most common – is to accept and follow anti-doping regulations.

That athletes are unable to opt-out of a system that, as above, has implications for their privacy and are expected to simply accept this as the price of being an athlete, reflects cultural values and understandings of what sport is, who should be allowed to participate, and the expectations for those who do so. Athletes who show less than perfect acceptance of the system are immediately suspect, while those who do not comply are banned from sport. It also shows the tension between how sport is valued compared with the value assigned to athletes. Sport must be protected, but only some athletes – "clean athletes" – are worthy of the same consideration. Even those protected athletes must still abide anti-doping, regardless of the fact that anti-doping can be oppressive to all athletes.

Questioning Hegemony: WADA Vs. The U.S.

To better illustrate how hegemony functions in sport governance, we can look at a challenge presented to WADA's hegemony by the United States. Using this case, we can see how hegemony is powerful and stable, yet never complete. This leaves hegemonic patterns, values, and actors open to resistance from other actors trying to bring about change. This case also shows how power clashes between actors with two different positions and types of power – here, the U.S. government and WADA as a non-governmental organization – can reshape some things while still retaining the same broad pattern.

As noted above, anti-doping is very much a top-down and WADA-led endeavor for much of the sport world. In general, WADA makes anti-doping policies that are then implemented and enforced through the broader anti-doping network of stakeholders. Through their agreements (consent) to join the anti-doping system and the broad cultural acceptance of WADA's agenda, these stakeholders are expected to comply with the Code. Each act of compliance by any stakeholder works to reinforce WADA's position as the moral leader on anti-doping. But not all stakeholders are created equal, and some are in strong positions to challenge WADA's position when they are dissatisfied.

National governments are one of the key stakeholder groups that can legitimately challenge anti-doping, including WADA as the lead organization. Most national governments signed onto the anti-doping system via the UNESCO Convention. However, as noted above, WADA retains no legal authority over states and instead relies on its moral authority and consent to its leadership role. Indeed, national governments are important to WADA's survival as an organization by providing it with half of its annual operating budget and the requirement that NADOs are set up and supported by individual countries. Countries that contribute more to anti-doping would then likely have more leverage over WADA. The U.S.'s 2019 contribution to WADA, for example, made up nearly 14% of its budget (Pells 2019). The loss of that amount of funding could potentially cripple parts of its operation and stall its agenda, as well as raise questions about its legitimacy and viability as the global leader in anti-doping.

One key challenge to WADA arose in 2019 when the U.S. introduced and then passed the Rodchenkov Act. This law, named for the Russian anti-doping lab director turned whistleblower Grigory Rodchenkov, gives the U.S. power to pursue criminal penalties against doping conspirators at international competitions or events – at any sport event where U.S. interests are represented, including those not held in the U.S. – under criminal law. This law posed two direct challenges to WADA and its hegemony: (1) it attempted to relocate power to adjudicate international anti-doping cases to the U.S. and attempting to regulate anti-doping in the international sport realm, and (2) it sought to put U.S. national interests above those of sport when it came to anti-doping.

The first challenge was a question of jurisdiction since international anti-doping cases had been left to WADA up until the Rodchenkov Act. Previously, each NADO was responsible for carrying out anti-doping functions within the country, and national governments could pass laws in support of these efforts. In both cases, however, these powers stopped at the national border. Further, most countries had been happy to have anti-doping cases and issues handled and decided within sport structures. As the global anti-doping policy leader and the organization responsible for harmonizing anti-doping policy between countries, WADA has maintained oversight of cases across countries and could appeal decisions made by international federations or NADOs to the Court of Arbitration for sport. This means WADA can ensure policies are being enforced in line with its agenda, and each decision in its favor further stabilizes its hegemonic position and the anti-doping system as a whole. However, the U.S. government, with the support of its NADO, the United States Anti-Doping Agency (USADA), sought to upset this position to some extent by bringing international competitions and actors under its purview and into the national criminal justice system. WADA opposed this law in both public statements and its lobbying efforts, as did other countries and sport stakeholders. WADA wanted to avoid a situation where various countries used extraterritorial legislation to attempt to gain control over anti-doping, potentially setting up clashes between countries or between it and national governments. The latter is particularly important for WADA's position, as it has no control over national laws and its own policies can only be implemented within the limits of national laws.

The second main challenge to WADA was the changing of the hierarchy of values and interests related to anti-doping policies. As the Code is ostensibly based on upholding sport values, other values or aims are held as secondary. However, the Rodchenkov Act explicitly puts U.S. national interests above those of the greater sporting good. While there are overlaps between the two, the U.S. law supersedes the Code and in any policy clash, the U.S. will win out and its interpretation or decisions will be the rule rather than WADA's. Indeed, one of the critiques leveled at WADA by USADA and other U.S. stakeholders was that WADA had been too weak in holding Russia accountable following the revelations of its state-sponsored doping program and had failed in governance reforms. One of the Rodchenkov Act's sponsors in the Senate, Senator Sheldon Whitehouse, proclaimed:

> The responses of WADA and the International Olympic Committee to the Russian doping scandal fall woefully short. Now is the time to create stiff penalties for Russia's cheating and send a signal that Russia and other sponsors of state-directed fraud can't use corruption as a tool of foreign policy. ("Whitehouse" 2019).

By reframing what had been largely considered a sport issue as a question of foreign policy, anti-doping was situated outside the realm of sports and therefore beyond WADA's narrower jurisdiction. The U.S. even went so far as to threaten withholding its funding to WADA in order to make its point about the agency's ineffectiveness (Brown 2020). The head of USADA, Travis Tygart, accused WADA of allowing itself to be bullied by Russia at the expense of sport values when offering his rationale and support for the Rodchenkov Act. In short, this critique allowed the U.S. to use anti-dopism as a weapon against WADA in order to expand its own influence within anti-doping. This directly threatens WADA's moral authority and leadership, calling its hegemonic position into question and opening the possibility for another actor – USADA – to step in and take over.

WADA recognized this challenge and responded by criticizing the U.S. and USADA for overstepping and seeking to try to replace the (nominally independent) WADA with its own leadership that would likely prioritize its own interests. In response to its threat to withhold funding, WADA countered with a threat to find the U.S. non-compliant with the Code and potentially jeopardize its bid to host a future Olympic Games. Current WADA

President Witold Bańka noted that USADA seemed to be trying to purchase influence and, failing that, simply seize control of anti-doping through efforts like the Rodchenkov Act. In an open letter he noted that WADA had been attacked politically, but that "I will not allow WADA to get bogged down in these political games; and that control of WADA is not for sale, no matter what stakeholder we are dealing with" (Bańka 2020). Despite WADA's opposition, the U.S. adopted the Rodchenkov Act as a national law in 2020.

As this example shows, hegemony is powerful and often stable, but never complete. It is always open to challenge and resistance. WADA's position is weakened in the absence of consent by its partners, cooperation in achieving its aims, and stakeholder compliance with its goals. It relies on these softer forms of power since it lacks the traditional forms of power normally reserved for states (i.e., police, power to make binding laws, etc.). When challenged by states that do have those powers, then, WADA has little recourse apart from moral appeals to follow its agenda. Even with support of other countries and sport federations, WADA is virtually powerless to prevent a country from undermining its policies and approach.

Anti-Dopism, Global Dominance And National Resistance

Looking at institutions and systems can help us understand how values and views are transmitted and who is responsible for doing so. Hegemony, however, can help us understand how institutions can successfully formulate, control, and direct particular narratives and how these can become widely – even globally – accepted. WADA was able to pick up on broader sport values related to

Olympism and use those as the rationale for its main aim of eliminating doping in sport. WADA was created through an agreement between national governments and the IOC and has since relied on cooperation with these stakeholders to enact policies and carry them out, primarily with the support of NADOs who help ensure compliance. Once it was empowered by countries and sport stakeholders to make global anti-doping policy, WADA leveraged this position to define doping and to direct the social and cultural narrative around doping by linking it to questions of morality and broader social fears of drug use. This also helped underpin its approach to anti-doping policymaking that focuses mainly on individual athletes by prohibiting substances and punishing athletes who fall afoul of these rules. Athletes must comply with these rules if they wish to participate in sport, while countries and sports federations have generally complied with WADA's agenda and policies. Together, these have reinforced WADA's hegemonic position as the moral and policy leader on anti-doping.

Though WADA has successfully maintained its position, it has not been without challenges to its power. As we showed in the case of the U.S., countries are well placed to resist WADA when they disagree with its approach or methods by simply passing laws that take precedence over WADA's policies. The U.S. successfully did this with the Rodchenkov Act over the objections of WADA and other stakeholders. Such a move by a country – especially one as powerful and important for anti-doping as the U.S. – was a blow to WADA's hegemonic position within the global sport governance structure. WADA was not toppled and it does remain the standard bearer and primary policy maker globally, but the U.S. did show that WADA is not immune to challenges to its position.

Despite this, it is important to note that even with WADA's weakened position, the hegemony of the anti-doping system and of anti-dopism remains fully intact. Though the way this plays out in terms of policy and WADA's position may be altered, the Olympic and sport values that underpin the current anti-doping approach have been reinforced. The U.S. going beyond WADA's own policies on the argument that they are too weak, actually strengthens anti-dopism as the current prohibitive and punitive approach. This is how hegemony can work through institutions: anti-doping narratives and the values associated with it remain and are even strengthened no matter which actor is making policies.

Discussion Questions

- What is anti-dopism?
- What would an alternative to WADA's cultural narrative of anti-doping look like?
- How is WADA able to maintain its hegemonic position despite not having powers reserved for countries?
- How does the U.S.'s adoption of The Rodchenkov Act challenge WADA's hegemony?

A link to access additional online resources is provided at: https://doi.org/10.18848/978-1-957792-21-7/CGP

CHAPTER 4

Conclusion

This book has presented theoretical ideas, interpretations, and applications of hegemony. Beginning with the work initiated by Antonio Gramsci, we traced the development of hegemony as both a concept and theory using gender in team sports and governance in anti-doping as examples of application. Though these applications differ from each other, and from Gramsci's original focus, the discussions have clear overlaps and align in a general sense. In both cases, the hegemony in question was situated in the crossroads between power and culture. Hegemony is heavily centered around power and culture, or power through culture. As such, hegemony as elaborated by Gramsci was also *cultural* hegemony. Hegemony describes how the value and ideals of one group – such as a ruling institution or organization, class, or gender – can come to dominate in a culturally diverse society. This dominance is made possible through the dominant group´s ability to direct beliefs, values, norms, and perceptions in that society. This gives primacy to their worldview, which is what they see as good or bad, more or less important, etc. The result is that this worldview achieves common consent and becomes the accepted cultural norm.

Hegemonic power differs, to some degree, from other types of power. It distinguishes between *productive* and *coercive* and authoritative power. The cluster of ideas around cultural hegemony do not focus on the various forms of authoritative power in society, through which rules, regulations, and even norms may be upheld by force if necessary. Of course, this form of power exists and continues to influence and direct the behavior of individuals, organizations, and even countries. Hegemony, though, is mainly about power that actively produces rather than represses. Hegemonic power is productive in the sense that it operates through consent to collective understandings of culture and cultural values.

Individuals, institutions, and countries are usually not explicitly forced to do anything by a hegemon or a hegemonic system. Hegemonic power may be reinforced by authoritative force, but it mainly relies on collective conformity with accepted cultural expectations. It operates through the ways individuals learn to strive for certain things, or to act in a certain way, and when certain things are taken for granted because they figure this is simply how things are. This conformity may also include active support for these norms and expectations, but it does not require it, and may be the result of a general tacit acceptance of the dominant group's ideals.

Looking at team sports as an area of application illustrated how both women's and men's notions of the athlete or athleticism are saturated in gendered understandings. As an athlete, one is supposed to show capabilities and skills such speed, strength, courage, being a team player, etc. These are the cultural values and ideals put forth. Interestingly, although these attributes individuals can live up to regardless if they are men or women, in most cultures they tend to be associated with men and masculinity. Men and masculinity have monopolized these competencies, creating a cultural narrative of the idealized team player as well as the gender of this player. As a result, men throughout history have been able to maintain their dominant role in sport and reap social, cultural, and economic benefits through sport participation. Women – and men failing to live up to such standards – have been questioned or received fewer or lesser benefits, such as being given less time in media, lower pay, etc.

Similarly, anti-dopism illustrated how WADA has been able to create a cultural narrative around the idea of clean sport and fair play. Their view has dominated the anti-doping debate and how anti-doping work has been organized and subsequently has had a significant impact on how doping in sport and society is currently understood. This hegemonic narrative is upheld through agreement with governments and the IOC, mainly relying on cooperation for legitimacy. Chapters 2 and 3 illustrated that even though cultural hegemony builds upon the "spontaneous consent given by the great masses," resistance and questioning also take place. To this end, consent and resistance coexist. Hegemony is not static; rather, it is the currently accepted cultural narrative that must be constantly negotiated and renegotiated.

How Can Hegemony Help Us Understand Power In Sport And Elsewhere?

As a theoretical concept, hegemony, like other concepts, works on multiple levels. At a rudimentary level it is simply vocabulary, just a word that can be translated or briefly explained. To be able to explain a word or concept means that we have a fairly good idea of what we are talking about. In this case, hegemony is a concept used to discuss how power and domination operate in culture and society. This level of explanation does not differ significantly from how we use and situate other words. In daily life, most people would probably know what the word "love" means, and maybe describe it in terms of a human emotion of affection; that one cares for something or someone a great deal. The first level of understanding provides direction and a sense of context. Concerning hegemony, we know that Gramsci was not the only one who had an interest in culture, power, and domination. Scholars such as Weber, Marx, and Foucault have approached this discussion in somewhat different ways, using other vocabulary and foci. So, the first level here would be to understand the focus of cultural hegemony and to situate this concept, knowing the contexts in which it can be utilized.

Moving on to the second level of understanding, we enter the field of analysis. Like love is an emotion that more easily understood in relation to a whole range of other emotions – care or dislike, affection or hate – theoretical concepts are similarly relational. Concepts need other concepts to produce meaning. In this way, hegemony as a concept in itself does not provide that many insights. It needs to be set in motion by other concepts. For Gramsci, cultural hegemony could be used to explain the relationship between culture and power in a capitalist society. Gramsci´s ideas clustered around this concept but were also paired with other concepts we have discussed: culture, power, domination, resistance, consent, and control.

Others then picked up and refined this concept, developing their own focus and understanding. Connell, for example, explained how one hegemonic form of masculinity could maintain its dominance in relation to lesser masculinities and women. Moving further still, Stuart Hall (1980; 1986) understood culture as being both produced and consumed simultaneously, making culture an active field where power is reinforced and challenged. Hall applied this to understandings of race and racism, among other topics, particularly focusing on the power of language. In a similar vein, Sara Ahmed (2006) examined whiteness and its relationship to anti-racism, arguing that the practice of ignoring race and realities related to it –sometimes part of white antiracism

– actually work to reinforce hegemonic whiteness. The point here is that hegemony needs to be paired with other concepts to reach an analytical level.

Consequently, when we use hegemony in tandem with other concepts we can analyze power relationships –such as the gendering of team sport or WADA's dominant position in international sport anti-doping. We can also begin to see similarities and differences between these different sites of application. When we have concepts in place and can describe how they are interrelated, we can also apply our theoretical frame to new areas, issues, or phenomena. This brings up the third level of use, which can be described as analytical transferability. This means that our theoretical framework in one area of application can be used to provide understanding of another.

At this third level of theoretical analysis, hegemony paired with other concepts can bring to light the very mechanisms in operation when power is maintained, questioned, and possibly resisted through culture. This third level is more abstract, where it becomes possible to see how similar mechanisms are at work in contexts that may seem to have very little in in common at first glance. Moving from men's locker room talk, to women football players' understandings of athleticism, to global ideals and values concerning anti-doping, we can see patterns that seem to repeat themselves. We can see and begin to explain these patterns when we examine them through the lens of cultural hegemony. Cultural hegemony, then, is a concept to describe power relationships and patterns, but it is also a theory that allows us to analyze those relationships and patterns.

When we have identified the mechanisms and patterns (level 2 and 3) and have a vocabulary for discussing them (level 1), it is possible not only to provide analysis of a particular phenomenon, but also to move between different areas of application. Basically, we can set the gendering of team sport and anti-doping aside and have a discussion on the matter at hand: power. We can debate how power operates through culture and ideals and see if our theory works to explain power dynamics in still other areas.

Hegemony At Work: Mechanism

Throughout this book we have gradually introduced central ideas for conducting an analysis of how power operates in the cultural sphere. We have established that this form of power can be described as productive and is characterized by cooperation and consent rather than the threat of force. At the heart of this discussion is the fact that certain cultural values, ideals and norms are set as broadly accepted defaults in a given context or society. As such, they set the standard for what to expect and what is valued. Even though it is not a given that individuals themselves will benefit from the outcomes of the culture they are part of upholding, still they tend to accept the explanatory logic of culture. Thus, they are part of upholding culture through agreement and consent.

Consent and *cooperation* are vital for cultural hegemony. It is through the ability to set cultural standards that the ruling group maintains its dominance. In contemporary culture, athletes largely share understandings concerning what constitutes a successful athlete and that the values of sport and morality are important to protect through WADA's global anti-doping efforts. Such values are often strong and may feel natural to the individual, even when they work against their own position. This type of tacit or unknowing consent reinforces the legitimacy of these power dynamics, as each act of consent works to uphold these powerful ideas. Despite how taken for granted hegemonic views may be, they are still cultural ideals and constructs, which may change over time and between cultures or societies. They may also be challenged.

Culture and cultural values are not carved in stone. Hegemony operates through consent but also includes *conflict* and *resistance*. Cultural narratives are constantly being rewritten, although often more in the fine print than in the main terms. Regardless of the fact that sport and muscles have been connected to men and masculinity throughout large parts of history, women's resistance to male dominance changed the conditions of sport participation. Today women can participate in sport, compete at a high level, and become professional athletes. These are all things that have only been possible relatively recently and came about through women's resistance to and questioning of their exclusion from sport. Still, however, men remain privileged. Here we see that conflicting interests can lead to resistance efforts to challenge the accepted order of things that may then bring about changes to dominant cultural understandings.

Hegemony, then, is about both stability and change. It is about how society and culture are upheld and how order and routine are created through shared understandings of cultural values. Consent to the cultural order brings about stability. But cultures and societies evolve and change over time. Life today is far different from one hundred, fifty, twenty, and even just ten years ago. What was once accepted as common sense may now be understood as completely old fashioned or irrelevant to contemporary life. Cultural change is often slow and incremental, due to the difficulty in challenging the norms set by socially dominant groups. Looking at the women's rights movement offers a clear example of this, as pushing back against policies, views, and behaviors that have benefitted men for centuries required years of challenge for often minor, yet important, changes. Though men still dominate many industries or areas of social life, the opportunities for women hardly resemble those of our parent's or grandparent's generations. And these challenges and changes to the status quo continue as the hegemonic gender order is constantly renegotiated.

The Hegemony Of Hegemony?

Hegemony has in some ways become hegemonic itself. In some areas, such as in cultural studies (see: Lash, 2007) and critical studies on men and masculinity, it was a dominant lens for analyzing how culture changed over time. We have reinforced this hegemony to some extent by writing this book – our consent to the view that hegemony is important for students to understand and use. But there are challenges to the utility, or even the legitimacy, of hegemony as a way to understand power, as well as to specific applications. Critiques of hegemony's application in some contexts provide alternative ways to understand and explain how power works at and across various levels. Some of these alternatives may compliment hegemony, but they may also pose a direct challenge the primacy this concept and theoretical approach has had in examining and explaining power. For example, within the field of critical studies on men and masculinity, scholars have sought to challenge and move beyond Connell's hegemonic masculinity (for example, see: Anderson 2009; Halberstam 1998). Still, within this field of research hegemonic masculinity maintains its place as an accepted way of understanding gender.

Hegemony is one way of looking at, analyzing, and explaining some forms of power. While this concept is useful, it is not the only way of analyzing or explaining power or dominant cultural patterns. Ultimately, hegemony's hegemony is incomplete and always up for challenge. Some have argued that while hegemony may have been useful in the past, new concepts and theories are needed to understand the increasingly connected and digital world as it currently is. In this context, the challenge comes from academics and theorists seeking alternative explanations for how the world works, including patterns of both stability and change and of cultural control and resistance. We encourage you to follow up this work with your own exploration of alternatives or complementary approaches to understanding power.

Discussion Questions

- What features of hegemony are visible in power relations across individual and socio-cultural levels?
- Outside of sport, where might we look to see if hegemonic masculinity functions in a similar way?
- What other examples of governance might reflect a hegemonic power dynamic between organizations, institutions, or countries?
- What other hegemonic beliefs or patterns impact your daily life? How?

A link to access additional online resources is provided at: https://doi.org/10.18848/978-1-957792-21-7/CGP

FURTHER INFORMATION AND READING

We recommend the following texts for those interested in further reading on hegemony, power, and culture; how the conceptual debate has developed in different directions; and applications in various contexts and topics.

Connell, Raewyn W. 1995. *Masculinities*. Cambridge: Polity Press.

If you are interested in hegemony and gender research, Connell's study on the social construction of masculinity is a classic. In her thinking, Connell used Gramsci's thoughts in combination with other thinking to develop her theory on hegemonic masculinity. She argued that many different masculinities exist and some of these are idealized while others are marginalized or subordinated. In this book, Connell showed how hegemonic masculinity can capture a gender order that privileges men over women, and some men over other men depending on which masculinities they are enacting. Although Connell has been criticized and others have aimed to challenge her theory, this theory remains fundamental within critical studies on men and masculinity. In the sport context, its contribution has been, and continues to be, highly influential in analyses of how gender and power operate.

Anderson, Eric. 2010. *Inclusive Masculinity: The Changing Nature of Masculinities.* **Routledge.**

This book provides a challenge to Connell´s concept of hegemonic masculinity. Anderson draws on his own experience of being a coach and coming out as gay around the turn of the twenty-first century to discuss culturalized violence against homosexuals and homosexuality in sport. When doing field work about ten years later, Anderson found evidence that suggested the homohysteria that he experienced himself has lessened and been complemented with an inclusive rather than domineering form of masculinity. Anderson suggested that gay men increasingly have been welcomed into the heteronormative world of sports. Further, he argued that an orthodox or traditional masculinity can coexist with a new form of inclusive masculinity, without any of them gaining a hegemonic position.

Andreasson, Jesper, and April Henning. 2021. "Challenging Hegemony Through Narrative. Centering Women's Experiences and Establishing a Sis-Science Culture Through a Women-Only Doping Forum." *Communication and Sport.* **Doi: https://doi.org/10.1177/21674795211000657**

This article focuses on an exclusive, women-only doping forum. It analyzes how issues related to doping use and gender are addressed by women when their views are not backgrounded by potential male commenters and misogynistic discourses. As such, the article address questions concerning resistance and what happens when women challenge patterns of hegemonic masculinity, setting their bodies and experiences as the standard and the unspoken norm.

Donnelly, Peter. 2015. "What if the Players Controlled the Game? Dealing With the Consequences of the Crisis of Governance in Sports." *European Journal for Sport and Society* **12, no. 1: 11-13.**

Sport governing bodies are often criticized for poor inclusion of athletes' views, as well as insular and opaque governance practices. This article focuses on various forms of hegemony that impact and shape sport governance. By looking at emerging sports, Donnelly looks at ways to resist some of the hegemonic patterns within sport and relocate and democratize sport power by putting it in the hands of athletes.

Lenskyj, Helen Jefferson. "Olympic Education and Olympism: Still Colonizing Children's Minds." *Educational Review* **64, no. 3 (2012): 265-274.**

In this article, Lenskyj took a critical view of the hegemony of Olympism in educational settings. She analyzed materials produced in several countries to examine how these disseminate Olympic values as a way of preserving the Olympic industry's hegemony. She argued that corporate messaging woven into such materials were overshadowed by the taken for granted view of Olympic ideals as important for moral development and laid out recommendations for resisting this hegemonic view.

BIBLIOGRAPHY

Ahmed, Sara. 2006. Declarations of Whiteness: The Non-Performativity of Anti-Racism. *Meridians: Feminism, Race, Transnationalism* 7, no. 1: 104–126.

Anderson, Eric. 2002. "Openly Gay Athletes: Contesting Hegemonic Masculinity in a Homophobic Environment." *Gender & Society* 16, no. 6: 860-877.

Anderson, Eric. 2010. *Inclusive masculinity: The Changing Nature of Masculinities*. New York: Routledge.

Andreasson, Jesper. 2007. *Idrottens kön. Genus, kropp och sexualitet i lagidrottens vardag* [*The Gender of Sports. Gender, Body and Sexuality in Team Sports Everyday Life*]. Lund: Sociologiska institutionen.

Andreasson, Jesper and Thomas Johansson. 2019a "Negotiating Violence: Mixed Martial Arts as a Spectacle and Sport." *Sport in Society* 22, no. 7: 1183-1197.

Andreasson, Jesper and Thomas Johansson. 2019b. "Bodybuilding and Fitness Doping in Transition. Historical Transformations and Contemporary Challenges." *Social Sciences* 8, no. 3: 80.

Bańka, Witold. 2020. "WADA President's Open Letter to Athletes." Accessed on January 20, 2022. https://www.wada-ama.org/en/media/news/2020-09/wada-presidents-open-letter-to-athletes

Barnett, Michael, and Raymond Duvall. 2005. "Power in International Politics. " *International Organization* 59, no.1: 39–75

Billington, Rosamund; Sheerlagh, Strawbridge; Lenore Greensides; and Anette Fitzsimons. 1991. *Culture and Society. A Sociology of Culture*. Basingstoke: Palgrave Macmillan.

Brown, Andy. 2020. "US May Withhold WADA Funding Due to Failure to Reform." *Sports Integrity Initiative*, June 24, 2020. https://www.sportsintegrityinitiative.com/us-may-withhold-wada-funding-due-to-failure-to-reform/

Burstyn, Varda. 1999. *The Rites of Men. Manhood, Politics, and the Culture of Sport*. Toronto: University of Toronto Press.

Connell, Raewyn W. 1995. *Masculinities*. Cambridge: Polity Press.

Connell, Raewyn W. 2000. *The Men and the Boys*. Berkeley: University of California Press.

Connell, Raewyn W. 1987. *Gender and Power. Society, the Person and Sexual Politics*. Cambridge: Polity Press.

Dahl, Robert. A. 1957. "The Concept of Power." *Behavioral Science* 2, no. 3: 201–215.

Dimeo, Paul. 2007. *A History of Drug Use in Sport 1876–1976. Beyond Good and Evil*. London: Routledge.

Fontana, Benedetto. 2008. *Hegemony and Power in Gramsci*. London: Routledge.

Foucault, Michele. 1979. *Discipline and Punish: The Birth of the Prison*. London: Penguin.

Foucault, Michele. 1980. *Power/knowledge: Selected Interviews and Other Writings 1972-1977*, New York: Pantheon.

Gallarotti, Giulio M. 2011. "Soft Power: What it is, Why it's Important, and the Conditions for its Effective Use," *Journal of Political Power* 4, no. 1: 25-47.

Gaston, Lindsey, Milly Blundell, and Tom Fletcher. "Gender Diversity in Sport Leadership: An Investigation of United States of America National Governing Bodies of Sport." *Managing Sport and Leisure* 25, no. 6 (2020): 402-417.

Halberstam, Judith. 1998. *Female Masculinity*. Durham: Duke University Press.

Hall, Stuart. 1980. "Race, Articulation and Societies Structured in Dominance." In *Sociological Theories: Race and Colonialism*, edited by UNESCO, 305-45. Paris: UNESCO.

Hall, Stuart. 1986. "Gramsci's Relevance for the Study of Race and Ethnicity." *Journal of Communication Inquiry* 10, no. 2: 5–27.

Hargreaves, Jennifer. 2000. *Heroines of Sport. The Politics of Difference and Identity*. New York: Routledge.

Hambrick, Marion E., Jason M. Simmons, and Tara Q. Mahoney. 2013. An Inquiry into the Perceptions of Leisure-Work-Family Conflict among Female Ironman Participants. *International Journal of Sport Management and Marketing*, 13(3/4), 173–199.

Haugaard, Mark, and Howard H. Lentner. (Eds). 2006. *Hegemony and Power. Consensus and Coercion in Contemporary Politics*. Lanham/New York: Lexington Books.

Henning, April, and Jesper Andreasson. (2022). "There´s a new sheriff in town." The Rodchenkov act, anti-dopism, and the hegemony of WADA in international sport. Sport in Society. 25(6), 1160-1175, Doi: 10.1080/17430437.2022.2064100

Hjelm, J. 2004. *Amasoner på planen. Svensk damfotboll 1965-1980 [Amazons On the Field. Swedish Women's Football 1965-1980]*. Umeå: Boréa Bokförlag.

Hoare, Quentin, and Geoffrey, Nowell Smith. (Eds). 1999. *Selections of the Prison Notebooks of Antonio Gramsci*. London:

Lawrence & Wishart.

Howson, Richard, and Kylie Smith. (Eds). 2012. *Hegemony. Studies in Consensus and Coercion.* London/New York: Routledge.

Kidd, Bruce. 2013. "Sports and Masculinity." *Sport in Society* 16, no. 4 (2013): 553-564.

Lash, Scott. 2007. "Power After Hegemony: Cultural Studies in Mutation?" *Theory, Culture & Society* 24, no. 3: 55-78.

Lears, TJ Jackson. 1985. "The Concept of Cultural Hegemony: Problems and Possibilities." *The American Historical Review*: 567-593.

Magrath, Rory, Jamie Cleland, and Eric Anderson (eds.) 2020. *Palgrave Handbook of Masculinity and Sport.* Basingstoke: Palgrave Macmillan.

Marx, Karl. 2013. *Manifesto of the Communist Party.* New York: Simon and Schuster.

Marx, Karl, and Friedrich Engels. 2009. *The Economic and Philosophic Manuscripts of 1844 and the Communist Manifesto.* New York: Prometheus Books.

McGrath, Shelly A., and Ruth A. Chananie-Hill. 2009. "Big Freaky-Looking Women: Normalizing Gender Transgression Through Bodybuilding." *Sociology of Sport Journal* 26, no. 2: 235-254.

Messner, Michael A. 1990. "When Bodies Are Weapons: Masculinity and Violence in Sport." *International Review for the Sociology of Sport* 25, no. 3: 203-220.

Mosse, George. 1996. *The Image of Man. The Creation of Modern Masculinity.* Oxford: Oxford University Press.

Pells, Eddie. 2019. "US Gov't Rep Unhappy with WADA Lobbying Effort." AP News, Accessed November 7, 2019. https://ap-news.com/article/3a8fe41d43414de1878805bf102456ca

Rowe, David. 2004. "Antonio Gramsci: Sport, Hegemony and the National-Popular." In Richard Giulianotti (Ed.), *Sport and Modern Social Theorists*. Basingstoke: Palgrave Macmillan.

Ruseski, Jane E., Brad R. Humphreys, Kirstin Hallmann, and Christoph Breuer. 2011. "Family Structure, Time Constraints, and Sport Participation." *European Review of Aging and Physical Activity* 8, no. 2: 57-66.

Taniguchi, Hiromi, and Frances L. Shupe. 2014. "Gender and Family Status Differences in Leisure-Time Sports/Fitness Participation." *International Review for the Sociology of Sport* 49, no. 1: 65-84.

Weber, Max. 1962. *Basic Concepts in Sociology*. Charleston: Citadel Press.

Weber, Max. 2009. *The Theory Of Social and Economic Organization*. New York: Simon and Schuster.

Whitehouse, Sheldon. 2019. "Whitehouse, Wicker, Jackson Lee, Burgess Introduce Rodchenkov Act." Accessed on January 20 2022. https://www.whitehouse.senate.gov/news/release/whitehouse-wicker-jackson-lee-burgess-introduce-rodchen-kov-act

Williams, J. Patrick. 2011. *Subcultural Theory. Traditions and Concepts*. Cambridge: Polity Press.

Zubizarreta, Ekain, and Julie Demeslay. "Power Relationships Between the WADA and NADOs and Their Effects on Anti-doping." *Performance Enhancement & Health* 8, no. 4 (2021): 100181.